COMIC ART PROPAGANDA

COMIC ART PROPAGANDA

A Graphic History   Fredrik Strömberg

ST. MARTIN'S GRIFFIN
NEW YORK

COMIC ART PROPAGANDA

For information, address St. Martin's Press,
175 Fifth Avenue, New York, N.Y. 10010.

www.stmartins.com

Library of Congress Cataloging-in-Publication Data
Available Upon Request

ISBN-13: 978-0-312-59679-8

This book was conceived, designed, and produced by
I L E X
210 High Street
Lewes, East Sussex
BN7 2NS
www.ilex-press.com

For Ilex:
Publisher: Alastair Campbell
Creative Director: Peter Bridgewater
Managing Editor: Nick Jones
Editor: Ellie Wilson
Commissioning Editor: Tim Pilcher
Art Director: Julie Weir
Senior Designer: Emily Harbison
Designer: Richard Wolfströme

First U.S. Edition: August 2010

10 9 8 7 6 5 4 3 2 1

Printed in China

Contents

This is not a comic.

This is not  a pipe.

This is not  misleading.

This is not  sexist.

This is not  racist.

This is not  unhealthy.

This is not  false.

This is not  proselytizing.

This is not  art.

This is not  THE END

with apologies to Magritte

Peter Kuper

This is Not a Foreword

After careful perusal of the material herein, I have but one message to convey:

DO NOT READ THIS BOOK.

It contains subject matter like SEX, drugs, religion, politics, and *SEX*. Worse still, they are all presented in the form of multi-paneled cartoons—a medium obviously for children, but in the examples presented here, blatant, unadulterated propaganda.

Propaganda, as we know, is from the Latin—*pro*, meaning *for*, and *paganda*, meaning *indoctrination of young minds*. (If you don't believe me, look it up.*) With his book, *Comic Art Propaganda*, Fredrik Strömberg has excavated a dizzying number of examples that demonstrate just how much that Latin word lives up to its promise.

Maybe it's so that "Truth is stranger and a thousand times more thrilling than fiction" (as the cover of the 1944 *True Comics* proclaimed in its subtitle), but lies are a hell of a lot more interesting, and Mr. Strömberg has dug up some whoppers! According to his examples, war is fun and bloodless, marijuana leads to madness, and having an abortion will send you straight to hell. But wait, also included here are comics that suggest our leaders don't have our best interests at heart, religion is the opiate to avoid, and sex, drugs and rock 'n' roll are a blast.

"POW! BLAM! ZAP! Comics aren't just for kids anymore" has been the mantra of a mountain of articles on this medium, but could it be that comics haven't been *just for kids…* ever? With tremendous insight and wit, Strömberg elucidates that this art form is not only a perfect vehicle for delivering potent messages, but also has the capacity to intelligently address any subject cartoonists are willing to explore. Comic books, like other literary forms, can tell the truth or lie, be for children or for adults, be clumsily scrawled or brilliantly executed. Their quality depends solely upon the skills and intent of the artist and their value is in the eye of the beholder.

Thanks to *Comic Art Propaganda*, now you can enjoy a guided tour across this art history and meet *Hansi: The Girl Who Loved the Swastika* as well as *Abortion Eve*. See *Grenada (Rescued from Rape and Slavery)* and encounter Auschwitz through the account of a survivor. Learn from one generation *Crime Does Not Pay* and from another the joys of drug dealing with *The Fabulous Furry Freak Brothers*.

Even those familiar with the form will encounter a wealth of surprises in this volume. Those who have never thought that comics could tackle everything they hold near and dear are in for a shock.

For everyone, this is a solid reminder not to believe everything you read— especially in forewords.

—Peter Kuper

* Don't look it up, like many of the comics in this book, I'm lying.

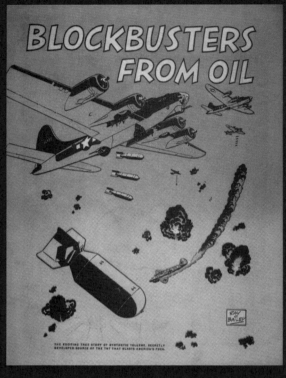

◄◄ This comic book was produced during WWII by the Standard Oil Company to inform Americans that the oil companies were responsible for the bombs dropped during the war. On the cover, you can read: "The Exciting true story of Synthetic toluene, secretly developed source of the TNT that blasts America's foes."

◄ Russian leaflet from 1941, handed out to strengthen the morale of the people during WWII. The text says, "Napoleon was freezing. Let's heat things up for Hitler."

◄ A recent example of the power of comic art is the worldwide controversies created by the so-called "Muhammad cartoons," which were published by a Danish newspaper in 2005. Here the Canadian cartoonist J. J. McCullough gives his view of the affair, a statement that also can be seen as propaganda.

◄ An article from 1942, published by the Nazi Propaganda Directorate, using an anti-Semitic Western comic from 1909 to show that Jews had taken over the U.S. The title translates to *"A Farsighted Englishman. The Domination of the Jews Will Be Brought to an End!"*

▲ The character Popeye was used in a series of comic books in the early 1970s to teach young people to choose the "right" careers. There were a total of fifteen different comics in King Features' Career Educational series, which were sold directly to schools in order to reach the target audience.

Propaganda and Comics!

Comics that tell you to join a fascist movement, adopt a new faith, or start hating your neighbor for the color of his skin? Surely such things don't exist. Comics are those lighthearted stories for kids, with bunnies in them. Right?

Wrong! Comics have been used time and time again as tools of propaganda. And why? Because comics have an almost magical way of catching and keeping the reader's attention. Survey after survey has shown that the comics section is the most well-read part of any daily newspaper. Is this because the comics are better written, more interesting, or more exciting than the rest of the content? Not to disparage the comics, but I don't think so. Or at least, that is not the only explanation.

I have spent almost two decades trying to understand the magic of comics, to work out what it is that makes comics almost hypnotic in the way they catch the eye and keep the reader enthralled. The intimate combination of words and pictures is one explanation. Speech balloons, captions, onomatopoetic words, etc. tend to give life and meaning to what might otherwise be lifeless images. Another explanation—and my favorite—is that the combination of two or more images forms a sequence, leading the eye across the paper, never giving the reader a chance to stop. A third explanation is that the iconic, simplified way in which many comics display their images is inherent in the way we view the world and thus speaks very directly to the reader.

Whatever the reason, comics have proven their power to fascinate. And this power has often been used with the express purpose of transmitting ideas and convincing the reader of various things, i.e. as tools of propaganda.

It should be stated that I view the term "propaganda" as more or less neutral. Indeed, propaganda was for a long time a neutral term, until it was used just a bit too arduously during World War II to sell the ideas of fascism and Communism by, respectively, the Nazis and the leaders of the Soviet State. Since then, propaganda has usually been seen as something bad. *The Oxford English Dictionary* defines propaganda as "any association, systematic scheme, or concerted movement for the propagation of a particular doctrine or practice." Moreover, it adds that the propagation of information is carried out "by an interested party, esp. in a tendentious way in order to encourage or instill a particular attitude or response."

That I do not look upon the term propaganda as negative in itself means that I have not only been looking for examples of comics being used to disseminate "bad" information (even though I started this introduction by enumerating some that I think are pretty bad). Rather, I have looked for comics that in some way try to transmit ideas to the reader, good or bad. This means that I have, for instance, included comics used to promote more "wholesome" ideas from democratically elected governments, comics designed to sell various products, and so on, not just easily condemned, atrocious comics that try to persuade readers to do or think things that most people would deem unacceptable.

When doing my research and choosing comics to show in this book, I have delved deep into my own comics library, which is extensive and contains examples from all over the world. Even so, a majority of the examples are from Anglo-Saxon countries, as these have been most easily accessible. Whenever possible, I have added examples from other parts of the world, to show that the use of propaganda in comics is not solely a phenomenon from the English-speaking world.

► A self-explanatory comics page by David Alvarez, done for the book *9/11: Artists Respond, Volume One*, which was published after the attack on the Twin Towers in New York.

► *The March to Freedom: The Birth of the Indian National Congress* is a comic from India that shows in excruciating detail how the British mistreated the Indian people, and how this led to the uprising and expulsion of the oppressors. A comic created to raise awareness of the past and strengthen the feeling of community among the various groups of people that make up India.

A limitation that I have imposed is to do my research mainly in the field of comics, and not include cartoons, animation, posters, and other closely linked art forms—which of course have also been used for propaganda purposes. Even so, when these art forms interact with comics, as for instance when comics artists have drawn propaganda posters or when comics characters have been used as insignia for battalions of war, I have sometimes chosen to include them as well. Thus the title of this book: *Comic Art Propaganda*.

Another question that arose: from what era should I collect my samples? At what juncture the art of comics emerged is a hotly debated topic (well, among comics historians anyway). Humans have drawn and told stories for as long as we know, so where you choose to start the history of comics depends on how you define this art form. For this book I have chosen to focus on the twentieth and twenty-first centuries. That is not to say that there aren't any comics older than that, or that they weren't used as propaganda for that matter. I simply had to restrict myself in order to make the book accessible and informative, and not just a long list of propaganda comics throughout the ages. My ambition has been to create a visually appealing and interesting book, not an academic study.

I have divided the examples shown into seven chapters, based on what the comics have been used to propagate:

In the first chapter, Us Versus Them, I look at comics promoting the idea that there are fundamental differences between groups of people. Or to put it frankly: racism—an area where it is, sad to say, very easy to find really horrible examples in comics. To contrast this, I also show examples of how comics have been used to confront racist ideas.

During wartime, the use of propaganda is often intensified in order to strengthen the national identity and convey an image of the enemy as subhuman, worthy of both fear and loathing. The second chapter, War! What is it Good For?, focuses on this in general and more specifically on World War II—a war in which propaganda was used most fervently.

Another period when propaganda flourished was the Cold War, which is the theme for the third chapter: You Dirty, Rotten Commie Bastard! This could easily have been the subject of a whole book, as both sides used comics extensively to sell their ideological and political ideas.

Comics have also been used in more sedate settings, often to educate readers on how to live their lives. This is the topic for the fourth chapter, Social Seduction, where I show examples of comics trying to teach us not to drink, not to smoke, or how to shoot small furry animals.

In the fifth chapter, Religious Rants, I look closely at a part of society that is chock-full of people trying to convince you that their ideas are the right ones. The battle over our souls is fought between major and minor religions, and this has resulted in some pretty scary propaganda comics.

Another area where there are strong feelings about "how it should be" is human sexuality, which I cover in the sixth chapter: Sexual Slander. Here I show comics trying to convince readers of the importance of adhering to sexual norms, as well as comics trying to convey the right to be different.

The seventh and final chapter, Political Persuasions, is all about politics—where convincing people of your agenda is of the essence. Comics have been used extensively as a tool in politics, for good or for bad depending on your own convictions.

Well, that's about it. If you've made it all the way here, I congratulate you and invite you to sink your teeth into the more meaty parts of the book. Or as the makers of these comics would have said: "Go ahead and read! It's good for you!"

Fredrik Strömberg, 2009

◀ The graphic novel *Maus: A Survivor's Tale*, by the American Art Spiegelman, is one of the most influential works of art about the Holocaust. Shown here is a passage from the comic, in which Spiegelman himself discusses the message of his story.

◀ The comic *X-Men: Life Lessons* was commissioned by the Starbright Foundation, an American non-profit organization that helps seriously ill children. The story focuses on a young superhero who has suffered severe burns to the face and has trouble adjusting to life again.

▼ The so-called *Chick Tracts* are some of the most widely spread propaganda comics in the world. These evangelical comics are published by the American company Chick Publications and are famous for their fervent endorsement of fundamentalist Christianity and arduous condemning of other religions.

Powerman was an attempt to launch a successful comic in Africa. The basis for the main character and storyline were American (and that they were taken from Superman is quite obvious), and the creative team was British, consisting of Dave Gibbons and Brian Bolland.

Chapter 1
Us Versus Them

Racial Stereotypes in Comics

Racism in comics? Surely not! Well, many still consider comics a medium solely geared towards kids, and even though that is not the case, there are a lot of comics made directly for a young audience. The problem with younger readers is that they may not yet have had the time to build up an understanding of the world for themselves, and as a result may be impressionable and prone to accept what they are shown without critical thinking. If you are out to create propaganda, this is of course not a problem but an opportunity.

To treat another person differently based on his or her skin color, faith, or general geographic affinity is a phenomenon that, as far as we know, is almost as old as humanity itself. And regardless of how evolved we consider ourselves to be in the twenty-first century, one glance at any daily newspaper tells you that this is not something that is about to go away. Racism is part of our world, like it or not. Comics are made by artists working in our world, and it is reasonable to assume that what they show us is a good cross-section of what is going on, both in the actual real world and inside people's heads. Read enough comics from one period of time and place, and you get a pretty good picture of how life must have been.

This is one reason why racism pops up quite often in comics, especially in the older ones, but it is not the only reason. I would argue, racism seems to pop up more frequently in comics than in many other art forms. One reason why this might be so is that the creators working in comics often use visual simplifications in order to tell their stories. Comics are, in essence, a narrative art form, and to get that readable flow the images are often reduced almost to iconic simplicity. When an artist working with comics designs a character, he or she may use easily recognizable traits to get the general idea of that character across to the reader. But in doing so, it is very easy to resort to characteristics based on biased or even racist grounds.

Whatever the reason, it is not exactly hard to find examples of all kinds of biased, or even racist, depictions of "the other" in comics. Many have probably not been made as a conscious effort to create propaganda, but this only makes them all the more devious. As time has progressed and our society has evolved, racist images of some kinds have become less frequent, as others have grown to be more common, all depending on history. In this chapter I will show some pretty horrendous racist images of various groups of people, while focusing on three groups who have been subject to a lot of visual abuse in Western comics: Jews, Blacks, and Asians. I will also show examples of ways in which comics have been used to counter these racist images with more positive comics, made to propagate a more constructive understanding. These might seem easier to live with, but they are still, in my book, propaganda.

► The Irish cartoonist Pat comments on how the cartoonists of England used to distort the faces of Irish people in order to please their audience. The first image shows a famous London cartoonist sent to Ireland to do research for the "*London Illustrated Smudge,*" the second his Irish model, and the third his drawing. This example is from 1881.

◄ This publication was made for the European Union, and published in large numbers in all of the official languages. It contains humorous comics about integration and cross-cultural understanding within the EU.

◄◄ A very potent propaganda, from the American newspaper *Citizen*. The cartoon is commenting on the fact that in 1928 the President-elect, Herbert Hoover, took a seven-week-long goodwill tour to more than half the countries of South America, to give a new face to "Uncle Sam." That South America is shown as a subordinate, pretty young female says a lot about the thoughts concerning this continent at the time.

◄ A beautiful piece of propaganda, published by the American fundamentalist Christian publisher Jack T. Chick in 1998. In this publication you can learn that anyone who doesn't help Israel will suffer the curse that God promised Abraham and Jacob (the ancestor of the Israeli people according to the Bible): "I will bless them that bless thee, and curse him that curseth thee."

◄ A cartoon from the American satirical magazine *Puck* from 1882, by the artist F. Gratz. The cartoon comments on the fact that America, which was built by immigrants, was trying to stop the Chinese from entering and doing business. The row of wall builders consists of traditional stereotypes of the immigrant groups in America.

► This image, called *The Coming Man*, was taken from American magazine *The Wasp*, from 1881, and was drawn by the artist Keller. It alludes to the fear that the immigrant Chinese Americans were taking over markets and pushing the white Americans out of their jobs. In the accompanying article it says, "The unsophisticated Mongol, imitating, ape-like, his fellows of this country, attains a monopoly of the cigar and laundry business, and smiles a cunning smile of triumph at his discomforted rivals."

Background illustration Mort Walker tried in the early 1990s to introduce a Japanese character in his comic strip *Beetle Bailey*, as a way of widening the scope of the strip. The fact that he was called "Corporate" Joe Kashikoi, was given a "funny" accent, and stereotypically Asian features, made the readers react negatively and the character was ultimately dropped.

◄ Many of the stereotypical traits associated with Asians in the American press were done in order to show Asians as less than human. Here is an example from the American magazine *The Wasp*, in 1877, where a perverted version of the hotly debated theories of Darwin are used to show how a "Chinaman" is closely related to monkeys and pigs.

▲ The very offensive *How to Spot a Jap* was produced for the American military by Milton Caniff (*Terry and the Pirates*), and was included in the guidebooks that were handed out to the American soldiers leaving for Asia. This is a version published in the *Chicago Daily Tribune* to educate the American people.

The Yellow Peril

▶ In Europe, caricatures of Asians have not been as widely spread as in America, or as hotly debated. The Belgian comic *Lucky Luke* takes place in the wild west, and includes blatant caricatures of Chinese Americans (even though it should be added that all characters in *Lucky Luke* are equally caricatured). This example is from the album *L´heritage de Rantanplan* from 1973 and was drawn by Morris (Maurice de Bevere).

The relationship between Asia and America is complicated to say the least. Early on, the U.S. tried very hard to get an agreement with China, in order to gain access to that vast export market. This deal was signed in the 1840s, but what wasn't expected was the quick influx of immigrants to the U.S. from China, due to the gold rush that started a few years later.

Even though this immigration never really amounted to a big part of the American population (about 0.002 percent in 1880), these new inhabitants of the U.S. were easily recognizable and were soon blamed for the hardening economic trends and accused of stealing jobs from (white) Americans. This fear that a large number of Asians would fill the country with foreign culture and take jobs from Americans was called "the Asian question" or "the Yellow Peril," depending on the political beliefs of the writers at the time.

These thoughts resulted in treaties to stop immigration, and also in the image of the Chinese (and due to the pan-Asian stereotyping of the West, of all Asians) changing from a curious Orientalist approach to downright racist,

derogatory hate-based propaganda. Asian men were depicted as trying to monopolize certain markets: laundry, cooking, manufacturing of clothes, etc. Actually, these areas were filled with Chinese workers because they were among the only ones available to them, and this due to the fact that the Chinese were deemed unmanly and really only fit for women's work. The association with these "unmanly" jobs, as well as Asian men often being shorter than the average American, having long braids, and wearing long silk gowns, gave rise to the stereotype of the effeminate, almost emasculated Asian man.

Other stereotypical traits associated with Asian men were that they were misogynists and prone to be disrespectful towards women. They were also portrayed as predators of white women, an image used extensively during World War II when Japan became a military enemy. This was further added to when China became a major enemy during the Cold War. All of this further complicated the image of the Asian in America. But I will get back to the subjects of WWII and the Cold War later in this book.

Over the years it has become clear that the Asian minority in America is also the subject of a so-called model minority stereotype; that is to say, positive traits are applied as a stereotype. Asian Americans are believed to be hardworking, studious, intelligent, productive, and generally inoffensive (good traits, but terribly hard for the average Asian American to live up to). They are, in other words, good immigrants, stereotyped as being "better" than the African-American population in the U.S. On the other hand, they are still viewed, as a group, as outsiders, not being able to assimilate, in contrast with the black minority who are seen as "insiders." A lot of work has been done to change these notions using propaganda and even comics to counteract the above-mentioned stereotypes, but at the same time this stereotype is enhanced by popular culture, which still reproduces it over and over again.

Tintin and the Yellow Man

The Adventures of Tintin is one of the most popular European comics ever, with translations published in over fifty languages and more than two hundred million copies of the books sold to date. The main character in this humorous adventure comic, Tintin, is a rather neutral character surrounded by a cast of charismatic, energetic, and very idiosyncratic supporting characters.

The comic was created by the Belgian Hergé, pseudonym for Georges Remi, in 1929. Up until his death in 1983 he produced twenty-four *Tintin* albums. Early on in his career, Hergé was content to just make funny adventure stories, not bothering with research. Thus, the first four *Tintin* adventures, which saw him traveling to the Soviet Union, Congo, America, and Egypt respectively, were based on popular prejudices about these countries and are full of racist images.

In 1934 Hergé set out to create the fifth *Tintin* album, which was to take place in China. There was some fear that his depiction of China would be just as prejudiced as in the previous albums, and Father Gosset, chaplain to the Chinese students at the University of Leuven in Belgium, introduced Hergé to Zhang Chongren/Chang Ch'ung-jen (known to Hergé as Chang Chong-chen), a young Chinese art student at the Brussels Académie des Beaux-Arts. The two young men became friends, and Chang taught Hergé a lot about Chinese art, life, and society. In fact, he taught Hergé so well that *The Blue Lotus* turned out to contain one of the most correct European views of the time, not only of China, but of the whole political situation in Asia. This was at a time when the clouds were gathering before the storm that was to become World War II. Japan had occupied parts of Manchuria, but since Japan was an old ally of both France and Great Britain from World War I, everybody in Europe seemed to think that this was for the best.

Everybody? No, a small comics supplement in a Catholic children's magazine in Belgium dared to think differently! Hergé filled *The Blue Lotus* with comments on what was going on, and showed the Japanese occupation from the point of view

of the Chinese. For instance, Hergé depicts the Mukden Incident—when a train derailed as the result of an explosion and the Japanese blamed Chinese dissidents, using it as an excuse to invade—and has Tintin show that it was actually Japanese spies who blew up the railway. He also heavily criticizes the apologetic way in which the West viewed Japan's actions.

Hergé took great pains in showing the inhabitants of China/Manchuria as real people, not simply as racial stereotypes. There had been Chinese characters in both *Tintin in the Land of the Soviets* and *Tintin in America*, but they had been based on the prejudices in Belgium at the time: they had buck teeth, pigtails, were cruel and sadistic, and prone to eat dogs. In *The Blue Lotus*, the Chinese are shown as real people, not least the character Chang Chong-Chen, whom Hergé based directly on his Chinese friend. The Japanese, on the other hand, got treated pretty badly; so bad, actually, that Japanese diplomats made a formal complaint to the Foreign Ministry in Brussels.

The Republic of China, on the other hand, was so pleased with *The Blue Lotus* that the Great Leader Chiang Kai-shek invited Hergé for a visit. However, because of objections to the implied ideology of *Tintin*, the People's Republic of China forbade the publication of the album for a long time. When it was finally allowed publication in 1984, some controversial items were changed. For example, the Chinese words 抵制日貨 (Down with Japanese products!) were changed to 大吉路 (Great Luck Road). Not bad for a children's comic from Belgium to be censored fifty years later in another part of the world altogether!

▶ *The Blue Lotus* in the original, black-and-white edition, which contains even more heavy political comments than in the later, revised color version, which is the one more readily available today.

- HERGÉ -
The adventures of
TINTIN

THE BLUE LOTUS

CASTERMAN

▼ Here Hergé shows how the Japanese use an alleged attack on the railroad in 1931 as an excuse to invade Manchuria, and how the European politicians totally misinterpret the situation. This probably went over the heads of the young boys who were the intended readers of *Tintin*, but it is a pretty accurate description of the Mukden Incident, which had happened just years before this was printed.

◀◀ Not only did Hergé try to make all the Chinese characters in *The Blue Lotus* look like real people, he also employed the help of a Chinese friend to make sure that all the signs contained legible Chinese signs. For those who could actually read the signs, they contained messages of anti-Japanese propaganda.

◀ One of the covers of the magazine in which the weekly installments of *Tintin* were published. The image shows Tintin being prepared for beheading by a Japanese soldier, with the caption reading, "The execution will take place at dawn." Pretty heavy stuff to show in a Catholic magazine for boys in 1934.

▲ Here Hergé shows the folly of having unfounded prejudices about people from other parts of the world, and he did it not by having Chang recount "funny" ideas about Westerners, but by showing the strange ideas Europeans had about the Chinese.

Black Images

There have been some really horrendous portrayals of black people in comics over the years—portrayals which have been used more or less consciously as propaganda to transmit the idea of a race that is inferior in every sense of the word. If you look at the three big comics cultures in the world, the American, the Franco-Belgian, and the Japanese, there are some differences in how this has expressed itself.

In the U.S., where African-Americans make up about twelve percent of the population, black people have often been portrayed in comics, and stereotypical images of black people were fairly common up until World War II.

One can discern at least seven different basic black stereotypes that have been established in stories aimed at a predominantly white American audience. I might call the first stereotype simply—for want of a better word—the *native*, namely the unflattering portrayal of native aboriginals as childish savages, both silly and dangerous. Next comes the *Tom*, an eternally servile, humble, and forgiving soul who never questions the superiority of the white ruling class; his name derives from the traditional, if somewhat incorrect, popular reading of Harriet Beecher Stowe's title character in *Uncle Tom's Cabin*. The third stereotype is the *coon*—a roguish funny figure known for mischievous pranks and linguistic distortions; the fourth stereotype is the *piccaninny*—a younger version of the coon, susceptible to leaps of the imagination and "funny" over-enthusiasm. The fifth type is the *tragic mulatto*, particularly common as a topic for films: a person

▲▲ The Belgian comics creator Hergé was asked to do a story about the Belgian colony of Congo, which resulted in the album *Tintin in the Congo* from 1931. Later in life, Hergé commented that the story was made in the spirit of the times, when Belgians felt that "The Negroes are like big children; how lucky it is for them that we are there!" Here we see Tintin in the original version, teaching little black kids about their "fatherland" Belgium.

▲ In this part of a French print from the late nineteenth century, *The Adventures of Cyprien Grenouillot*, we see how an assistant apothecary dreams of traveling to faraway lands but gets a rude awakening when he finds out why the "savages" had fed him so well. The myth of cannibalism in Africa was perpetuated in popular culture in Europe in order to make the Africans seem even more savage and in need of Western influence.

▶ American comics from the beginning of the twentieth century are full of supporting black characters, almost always servile and in service to the white main characters, mirroring the state of the country as a whole. Here, an example from a Sunday page from 1928 of the comic *Moon Mullins* by Fred Willard.

(most often female) sexually torn between black and white worlds, her sensual nature making her an "acceptable" object for white desire even as her black legacy dooms her to tragedy. The sixth common stereotype is the *mammy*, a sort of feminine Tom—complete with large, ungainly, asexual physique and an unwavering loyalty to the white household for which she works. The seventh and final stereotype, the *buck*, is a strong, violent, and rebellious "bad Negro," most often used as a cautionary example.

These stereotypes functioned as easily accessible icons which could be used by the cartoonists as storytelling tools, and were expected to suggest to the reader certain associations such as servility, laziness, superstition, and so on.

In Japan, an extremely homogenous society, comics artists had little or no firsthand experience of black people, but were heavily influenced by American comics. It is thus not too uncommon to find some of the above mentioned stereotypes in Japanese comics from the first half of the twentieth century, used more or less without the knowledge of their historical background. This continued long after they had stopped occurring in American comics, and were not abandoned until a small group of black people in Japan started a campaign to have them removed from the comics.

In Europe, the question of black images in popular culture has not been as contentious as in the U.S., even if it is influenced by a collective guilty conscience stemming from colonial times. The stereotype blacks also remained longer in European comics, but were depictions of the native, rather than of black people from the cartoonist's own environment. Both France and Belgium, the two major comics producers of Europe, had colonies in Africa, and ideas and images from their experiences can be found in many comics.

All in all, it is obvious that these stereotypes show how a wide audience of (mostly white) people at the time looked at black people. It is also evident that these images were used as a collective tool of propaganda to strengthen the ideas of white supremacy and reinforce status quo.

▲ In *The Spirit* from the 1940s by American Will Eisner, the character of Ebony is by today's standards a very offensive use of the stereotype of the piccaninny. Eisner was later in life aware of the way he had portrayed Ebony as a racial stereotype, but at the time he probably only showed what many thought was a socially acceptable image of a black person.

The Golden Legacy
of Bertram A. Fitzgerald

◀ In the issue of *Golden Legacy* about the life and death of Martin Luther King, parts of King's most famous speeches are not only printed but very effectively told in comics form, in order to give the reader the truest sense of the words.

▲ In the comic about Alexandre Dumas, there is never any doubt as to the origins of this famous French author, as we get to follow his family all the way back to Haiti, where his mother and father lived.

There have been a number of more or less unsuccessful attempts at launching comic books with black heroes in America. For instance, Milestone Media made a valiant attempt in the 1990s, with titles like *Hardware*, *Icon*, and *Static*. Despite a favorable agreement with DC Comics, one of the major comics publishers, the attempt ultimately failed. Recently it has been announced that the Milestone characters will be incorporated into the DC universe, but whether they will be given individual titles remains to be seen.

The most successful American publisher of comic books geared towards a black audience was not Milestone but *Golden Legacy*, launched in 1966 by an accountant with no prior knowledge of publishing enterprises. His name was Bertram A. Fitzgerald, and growing up in Harlem he read and enjoyed *Classics Illustrated*, even though he sometimes had a problem identifying with their stereotypical portrayal of black people.

Later in life, when he realized that authors like Alexandre Dumas and Alexander Pushkin actually were black, something that was never mentioned in the biographies of the authors of *Classics Illustrated*, he started *Golden Legacy*—a series of comic books about the lives of real black heroes. Without any experience in writing, printing, or distributing comics, and having the additional "handicap" of being black and quite often being denied business deals on racist grounds, making *Golden Legacy* turned out to be a struggle for Fitzgerald. When he brokered a deal with the Coca-Cola Company as the main sponsors of

Golden Legacy, the tide turned and the comics were a hit. Coca-Cola actually bought substantial quantities of the comic books and distributed them free to schools and libraries, as well as through organizations like the NAACP (National Association for the Advancement of Colored People).

The comics portrayed a number of well-known African-American heroes as well as some more forgotten ones. We can read about Harriet Tubman, a former slave who led hundreds of other slaves to freedom through the so-called Underground Railroad, and the Civil Rights activist Martin Luther King. Among the lesser known are Crispus Attackus, who led the first American revolt against the British, and Matthew Henson, an American explorer and associate of the more famous Robert Peary, who in a 1909 expedition was actually the first to reach the Geographic North Pole. The series also contained issues about the lives of the authors Dumas and Pushkin—clearly showing their black heritage.

At the same time Fitzgerald was publishing these comics, which still hold up as well written, engaging stories, the publisher of *Classics Illustrated* tried to keep up and managed in 1969 to publish, as its last American edition, the comic *Negro Americans, the Early Years . . .*

Golden Legacy eventually ran for sixteen issues. The comics are still kept in print and can be ordered through Fitzgerald Publishing Co. The total number of issues of *Golden Legacy* sold exceeds nine million.

◀◀ In the story *Joseph Cinqué and the Amistad Mutiny*, the reader is presented with the tale of how a black man led a slave revolt on the Cuban ship Amistad in 1839, and ended up in an American court where the trial led to establishing the rule that slaves escaping from illegal bondage should be treated as free men.

◀ The covers to the *Golden Legacy* series were sedate and classical, designed to be accepted in schools and libraries during a time when comics were not exactly looked on favorably by those institutions.

I am Curious (Black)!

▶ An issue of the comic book *Lois Lane* from 1970 sported this daring cover. The content was, of course, indicative of the very year it was published, when racial issues were still at a boiling point in the U.S. The story was written by Robert Kanigher and drawn by Werner Roth and Vince Colletta.

▶▶ The (over)dramatic ending to the *Lois Lane* story, where an agitator for Black Power realizes that he has been saved by a blood transfusion from a white person. In the panel before this scene, Superman utters the following melodramatic line: "If he still hates you with your blood in his veins . . . There may never be peace in this world!"

America has, because of the country's history of slavery and racism, a troublesome past to process. This has been tackled in all kinds of ways, including in superhero comics.

For a long time, after World War II when racially insulting images of black people were no longer accepted, comics creators were bewildered as to how to treat this volatile subject, and for a period black characters almost totally disappeared from American comics. But in the 1960s, the winds of change had finally made it possible to address this theme, and consequently it was done again and again, often with some rather heavy pedagogical or propagandistic purpose—depending or how you look upon it—behind the curtains of these stories pretending to be just entertaining.

My favorite propaganda comic from this interesting time is an issue of the comic book *Lois Lane*, the (sort of) girlfriend of Superman, called *I am Curious (Black)!* This comic is from 1970 and is very indicative of the times in which it was produced. Lane is of course a reporter, and gets the brilliant idea to do a

story on the black parts of Metropolis (the imaginary city they live in, probably mostly resembling New York in this story). She is constantly avoided and shunned by the black population, and finally accepts the help of Superman, who uses the "Plastimold machine" to turn her into a black person for a day.

After this, Lane has no problem getting in touch with the inhabitants of "Little Africa," but she also suffers some mild forms of racism (OK, so she's only neglected by a taxi driver). The real clincher, though, is when an agitator for Black Power gets shot and the only one who can give him the right kind of blood is, of course, Lois Lane. When she reverts to her normal shape and confronts him, it all ends in understanding and love (not too much love, though, they only shake hands—that was obviously enough when it came to interracial interaction in 1970). A real tear jerker!

Another highlight from this period is an issue of *Justice League of America*, called *Man, thy name is—Brother!* from 1967. In this very politically

▼ The three most successful titles of the Milestone imprint, which was launched in 1993 to fill the gap of African-American superheroes within the American comics culture. Ultimately, the effort failed and all of the titles were canceled, but the impact on the comics business was notable and these titles reached a big audience while they lasted.

correct story, three members of the Justice League of America (a group of superheroes) help their mascot, young "Snapper" Carr, to do research for a term paper on Brotherhood week—a national event in the U.S. from the 1940s to the 1980s with the aim of fighting bias, bigotry, and racism, and promoting harmony between different groups.

The three unlikely heroes, the Flash, Green Arrow, and Hawkman, race around the world to meet three men who have all been the victims of racism: one black guy and a Native American boy in the U.S., and a white man working in India. All three are featured in short stories that are full of the very racist prejudice they are supposed to fight. The Native American (named Jerry Nimo . . .) turns out to be an expert at reading signs in nature and following tracks on the ground, and the Indians are a cowardly, superstitious lot, easily fooled by

▶ In the comic book *Green Lantern/Green Arrow* from the early 1970s, writer Dennis O'Neil and artist Neal Adams took on some pretty serious subjects, at least for a superhero comic. Here is a scene from the beginning of the story *No Evil Shall Escape My Sight!*, which dealt with racism and the inevitable failure of these spandex-clad superheroes to do anything about this widespread and thoroughly entrenched phenomenon.

Jewish Nose Jobs

The Jewish people have been subject to anti-Semitism for millennia, and the perpetrators of these hate-based thoughts and acts have used literature, art, and even comics to convey their religious, racial, cultural, and ethnic biases. In fact, anti-Semitism and the art of caricature have an intimately shared history. Some of the first caricatures known, in both English and German, represented Jews.

The image of the Jew has developed over a long period of time and distinguishes itself from many other xenophobic images by its persistence. Most of the stereotypes commonly used to denote that a character is Jewish stem from the Middle Ages. These are, in no particular order:

The Jew as a traitor and a manipulator, showing Jews to be devious and untrustworthy. These images are often symbolically referring to Judas, "the first Jewish traitor."

The Jew as an economic leech, personifying usury and modern capitalism. The most famous of them all is of course Shylock, the character from Shakespeare's play *The Merchant of Venice.*

The Jew as a skeptic and iconoclast, a revolutionary who undermines faith and authorities. This is often referred to as the Red Jew, often used together with the above stereotype and disregarding the contradiction in terms.

The Jew as a non-human or diabolical assassin, poisoner, and polluter. Here, traits otherwise associated with the devil are used to show that Jews should not even be treated as human beings.

The Jew as a sexually obsessive rapist and pornographer, and the Jewish woman as a temptress. These images were shown to scare the reader about the dangers of mixing with the Jewish "race," and thus polluting the pure blood of gentiles.

Comics and especially caricature are of course the perfect tools for anyone wanting to effectively slander a whole group of people. Over the years, a model of how to depict a Jew has developed.

Initially, Jews were shown in the special attire that was enforced in Europe after 1215. Adult male Jews had to wear a certain type of clothing while outside a ghetto (an area of a city designated only for Jewish inhabitants), in order to be distinguishable from everyone else. This included a white pointy hat, and in the caricatures a money pouch was also often added as a reference to the traitor Judas. When the racial debate took hold in the nineteenth century, Jews in the caricatures were depicted more and more as a separate race and were given all the traits that were at the time deemed unmanly—both physically and mentally. The Jews were portrayed with curly hair, an arrogant glance from heavy-lidded dark eyes, a crooked nose, thick lips, heavy, grasping hands, crooked legs, fallen arches, and so on. In short, the outward appearance of the Jew was supposed to reflect his inner self.

In Western comics and caricatures, these kinds of anti-Semitic depictions of Jews were common in the twentieth century up until World War II. This reflected the general opinions in the Western societies, where anti-Semitism was very much socially accepted. Looking through humor magazines from the nineteenth and early twentieth centuries, there is an abundance of these hate-based caricatures and comics with Jews as the intended targets. The Jews were the chosen "other," onto which a lot of the angst of the people was projected.

This seems to have changed when the full extent of the Holocaust was shown to the world after WWII, and a more nuanced debate about the Jews of the world was initiated. At the same time as anti-Semitic caricatures more or less disappeared from Western media, the conflict between the state of Israel and its Arabic neighbors has given rise to a new wave of derogatory Jewish images. I hesitate to call them anti-Semitic, since "Semite" is a term used to denote both Jews and Arabs, but it appears that the conflict between Israel and Palestine has given rise to inflammatory depictions of Jews throughout the Arab world.

Fünftes Capitel.

Kurz die Hose, lang der Rock,
Krumm die Nase und der Stock,
Augen schwarz und Seele grau,
Hut nach hinten, Miene schlau —

So ist Schmulchen Schievelbeiner.
(Schöner ist doch unsereiner!)

Er ist grad vor Fittigs Thür;
Kauwauwau! erschallt es hier. —
Kaum verhallt der rauhe Ton,

So erfolgt das Weitre schon.

Und, wie schnell er sich auch dreht,
Ach, er fühlt, es ist zu spät;

Unterhalb des Rockelores
Geht sein ganze Sach kapores.

▲▲ A recent cartoon, from the Qatar newspaper *Al-Watan* in 2008. It contains many of the old visual stereotypes for depicting a Jew: the crooked nose, the Star of David, the long beard, and the black clothes of the orthodox Jew.

▲ A German print from the fifteenth century, with the title *Das Grosse Judenschwein* (*The Great Jewish Swine*). To represent Jews with a non-kosher animal like the pig was a common way of making fun of the Jews in the Middle Ages. The Jews are here depicted with their easily identifiable pointy hats.

▶ A drawing from the cover of the French humor magazine *Le Rire* from 1898, by the artist Charles Léandre. The image had the title "Rothschild," which was an influential Jewish family who owned many banks, and implicates a Jewish conspiracy to conquer the world. This was published just around the time when the propaganda book *The Protocols of the Elders of Zion* was produced (see pages 32-33).

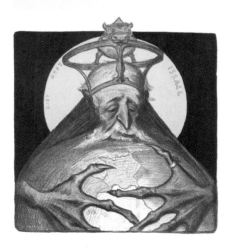

▲ A part of the picture story *Plisch und Plum*, by one of the most famous German cartoonists, Wilhelm Busch. The person being attacked by the two dogs is clearly Jewish, being described as having a bent nose, black eyes, and a gray soul. This fifth chapter of a popular story has often been deleted from later collected editions of Busch's work.

► *Shaloman #2 by Al Wiesner.* A beautiful piece of propaganda, where the hero not only defeats the Palestinian terrorist but also leads a group of well-trained, ninja-like Israeli soldiers in an attack on the evil genius who was really behind it all. Everything culminates in a scene that could have been taken from any James Bond movie, with Israeli soldiers mowing down the Arab henchmen who protect the villain's secret and highly sophisticated military base, as the hero goes after the bad guy himself.

▲ Al Wiesner's Shaloman is quite easily recognizable as a copy of Superman, and is even presented as "the Man of Stone" (as Superman is "the Man of Steel"). The fact that he reverts to the form of the Hebrew letter "shin" is probably because one of the interpretations of this letter is "God." A more famous usage of the letter in popular culture is the single-handed Vulcan gesture of Mr. Spock from *Star Trek*.

▲ Some dumbfounded Arab leaders from the comic book *Shaloman*. They are depicted with the easily recognizable plain, white keffiyeh of the Gulf state Arabs (which actually not everyone wears), and throughout the story shown as mumbling, stumbling buffoons confronted with the accuracy and ingenuity of the Israelis.

◄ The choice of words is important. Here an example from Stan Mack's *The Story of Jews*, a book about Jewish history, all done in comics form. The author tries to be objective and show all sides of an argument, as seen by the fact that PLO here is described as a "liberation organization" and not a terrorist organization.

▲▲ In David Gantz's book *Jews in America: A Cartoon History*, it is interesting to see that quite a lot of pages are used to tell the history of Israel. Whether this says something about the author's own views, or if it is indicative of the way the Jewish community in America looks upon Israel is debatable, but the views are not always all that neutral or objective—as can be seen for example in this sequence.

Shaloman & Company

The comics business in America is full of Jewish creators, editors, and publishers, and has been since the start—mostly because Jews were still barred from entering more fashionable areas of business and art in the beginning of the twentieth century when the art of comics took off in the U.S. So, even though many of the early Jewish creators had to change their names in order to get accepted, and steer away from too-obvious Jewish traits in their comics, not all depictions of Jews in American comics have been bad. Today the situation is quite different, and the creators do not have to hide their identity. Thus there are lots of openly Jewish comics, of which some can be seen as propaganda.

Of all the overtly Jewish comics I have read, *Shaloman: The Man of Stone* must be the most interesting from the perspective of propaganda. Made by the American Al Wiesner, who self-publishes a new issue about twice a year, it tells the story of the Jewish superhero Shaloman, a mystical being who normally takes the form of a stone carving of the Hebrew letter "shin" sitting atop Mount Israel. When something threatens the safety of (Jewish) innocents, he can be invoked by their cries for help—"Oi-vay!" (sic)— transforming into the spandex-clad form of Shaloman. This is told in the rather amateurish art of Wiesner, which is more sincere than well crafted.

The stories are mostly ordinary superhero stuff with Jewish themes thrown in, but sometimes they are more overtly propagandistic, like the story where Shaloman is called to the assistance of the Israeli prime minister because a "vigilante terrorist" called the Right Hand of Allah is killing settlers. Of course, our hero catches the terrorist, who—when his mask is removed—turns out to be the very same person who has pretended to work for the integration of Arabs and Jews on the West Bank. The rather ham-fisted moral of this story is evidently that Arabs in general are not trustworthy at best (and probably terrorists) and that any outstretched hand should be looked upon with

suspicion. It is, it has to be said, not too difficult to imagine that this can be extrapolated to include the overall peace negotiations between the Palestinians and Israelis.

Another highlight is the story where an evil genius uses a laser beam from a satellite to burn the ground solid in the oil wells of an Arab country. The leader of this country sends a representative to the UN, complaining that this must be the work of the Israelis. When asked for proof, the representative replies: "Well we . . . don't . . . exactly have proof! But-but . . . it took brilliant minds to do this! Logically—who . . . else could . . . it . . . be? Hmmm?"

There are other comics with clear Jewish themes that are not as obviously propagandistic as this, however. For instance, history books in the form of comics, like Stan Mack's *The Story of Jews* or David Gantz's *Jews in America: A Cartoon History*. They both present their stories as facts, which they are, given that both creators are American and Jewish and, like everyone, perceive the world in their own subjective ways. But so are most, if not all, history books, and a lot of them have through the years either just ignored the Jews or presented them as everything from degenerate pigs to the devil incarnate. Then again, show either of these two books to someone from Palestine, and they would be deemed as vile propaganda. It's all in the eye of the beholder.

Maus: It's a Cat Eat Mouse World

Of all the comics trying to deal with the difficult subject of the Holocaust, none have had as great an impact as *Maus* by Art Spiegelman. No other comic with such a serious theme has been as well read all over the world. In fact, *Maus* is arguably one of the most influential works of art about the Holocaust, ever.

Spiegelman tried out the idea in a few different versions in the early 1970s. The well-known version, which has been collected in book form, was created during a period between the late 1970s and the early 1990s, continually being published in Spiegelman's groundbreaking magazine *RAW*. For those few who haven't read *Maus*, it tells the story of the relationship between Art Spiegelman and his father, Vladek, a Holocaust survivor. The story follows their interactions and discussions, while at the same time graphically retelling the experiences of the father, a Polish Jew, who ended up in the Auschwitz concentration camp during World War II.

There are several reasons why I have chosen to include *Maus* in a book about propaganda. Spiegelman was, at the time when he started creating his masterpiece, making some of the most avant-garde comics in the world, comics that had more in common with art than with literature. Even so, when designing *Maus*, Spiegelman chose to use a more sedate, traditional way of telling stories, clearly in order to reach a wider audience. The pages of *Maus* rarely make use of the more expressionistic ways of visual storytelling that are available to a creator of comics. Rather, they tell the story clearly and with a literary feel, designed to appeal to a wide audience not necessarily acquainted with the latest styles of comics.

The use of anthropomorphic animals as characters in the story, something Spiegelman had not done very much before this, also makes *Maus* more accessible than if he had chosen a realistic style. By using symbolic and iconic animal characters, Spiegelman manages to tell quite horrendous stories without scaring the readers away.

◄ There are many comics dealing with the Holocaust, some more and some less propagandistic. The comic book *Judenhass* ("The Hate of Jews" in German) by the American Dave Sim, better known for the comic *Cerebus*, is one long propaganda statement about the persecution of Jews in general and during the Holocaust in particular, illustrated with drawings based on photos from the concentration camps.

If you compare the different versions of mice that Spiegelman used when he tried out various styles for the project, it becomes evident that he chose a very iconic look, especially for the mice, in order to make the reader identify with the Jewish characters.

Also, the use of the classic combination of cat and mouse gives the reader a ready-set interpretation of the relationship between the persecuted Jews and the authoritative German Nazis. This relates to ancient fables and children's stories, and to the real life relationship between these two groups of animals, but also to the fact that cats are big and carnivorous and mice are small, furry, and cute. It is also easy to see that the relationship humans have with mice—where the former often subject the latter to various ways of extermination—will affect the reader's interpretation of the story.

Taken together, it is evident that Spiegelman saw this story as special, and that he wanted it to reach and affect as many as possible, which it did. *Maus* is a classic, in the real sense of the word, and has reached millions of readers throughout the world. Is it propaganda then? In my book it is. Good propaganda, but still propaganda.

◄◄ *Maus* has been published in several different ways, initially in the magazine *RAW*, then as two volumes in 1986 and 1991, and finally as one single volume, which is how it is still being kept in print today. The book has been translated into a great many languages across the world.

◄ One of many horrifying scenes from *Maus*, which would probably not have been as effective and moving if it had been done in a more realistic style, with human characters instead of anthropomorphic ones. The use of mice, small and rather defenseless animals, as the persecuted Jews makes it even more obvious how to interpret what is happening.

► A very early version of *Maus*, from the underground magazine *Funny Aminals* (sic) in 1972. Here it is evident that Spiegelman had not yet come to the conclusion that the characters, and especially the mice, needed to be iconic-looking in order to engage the reader. In this version, the mice have a design that looks more like political caricature, which was probably the idea at the time.

►► In this dramatic and striking scene, Spiegelman shows us both the problem of using an anthropomorphic "mask" to show the Jewish identity of the characters, as well as the problem of making a story about something as atrocious as the Holocaust.

The Plot of the Protocols

► *The Plot* was the very last graphic novel made by the old master Will Eisner and for him a very important one, since it concerned a lie about the Jews. The book has since then sold well, but is still outnumbered by copies of the original Protocols by probably a thousand to one.

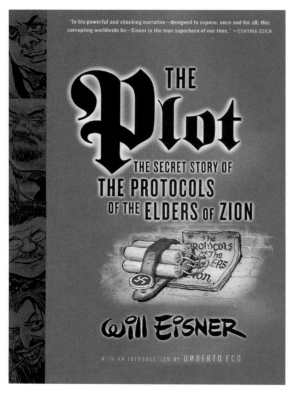

"In his powerful and shocking narrative—designed to expose, once and for all, this corrupting worldwide lie—Eisner is the true superhero of our time." —CYNTHIA OZICK

THE **Plot**

THE SECRET STORY OF
THE PROTOCOLS
OF THE **ELDERS** OF **ZION**

WILL EISNER

WITH AN INTRODUCTION BY UMBERTO ECO

Will Eisner was a legend in his own lifetime. He reinvented American comics at least three times, and he reinvented himself as a comics artist in the process.

Eisner began his career doing superhero comics for the burgeoning comic book market of the 1930s. When he tired of this he started the groundbreaking comic *The Spirit*, which ran as a sixteen-page comic book supplement to daily newspapers during the 1940s. After taking time off from the comic book market in the 1950s and 1960s, partly due to the massive criticism leveled at comics during that time, he managed a grandiose comeback in the late 1970s with the creation of one of the very first graphic novels, *A Contract with God*. He then proceeded to make at least one graphic novel a year, up until his death in 2005.

The last book Eisner ever created was a very special project. Eisner was Jewish, and even though this could not be shown (at least overtly) in the comics he made during the early stages of his career, it was very much a part of the stories he told when he started doing more serious work in the graphic novel format. His characters in these comics were often Jewish, and the stories took place in predominantly Jewish parts of America, often in his own childhood playground, the Bronx, a New York borough, which—at the time—was full of Jewish immigrants. Eisner never made a big deal out of the fact that his characters were Jewish, but rather showed them as believable people; people just like anybody else.

With his final book, however, Eisner took this theme even further, and did his first graphic history study, trying to put to rest once and for all the lies spread with the so-called *Protocols of the Elders of Zion*. The Protocols is a document put together in the late nineteenth century, purporting to be notes laying out plans for world domination and taken from a gathering of leading Jews. Even though this document has been proven a forgery many times over, it is still continually being published in new languages, and is constantly used to support anti-Jewish sentiments.

In the book with the rather cumbersome title *The Plot: The Secret Story of The Protocols of the Elders of Zion*, Eisner used all the skills he had acquired through almost seventy years of making comics professionally to prove to the reader that the Protocols were a forgery. He tells the story of how and why the Protocols were created, and also how they have been used to instigate anti-Semitism throughout the years since then. Eisner does this well, and after reading the book, there can be little doubt in the mind of the reader as to the fallacy of the document in question.

In the end, it is only fitting that such a well-made piece of propaganda as Will Eisner's *The Plot* was created to refute one of the most effective but sinister works of propaganda in modern times.

WHAT IF THERE APPEARED A DOCUMENT PROVING THAT MODERNIZATION WAS A PART OF A JEWISH PLOT?

IT WOULD BE **ABSOLUTE EVIDENCE** OF A THREAT THE **TSAR COULD NOT** IGNORE.

EXACTLY!

BRILLIANT, RACHKOVSKY! IT WILL MAKE WITTE'S ADVICE **SUSPECT!**

YES, IT WILL DAMAGE WITTE'S INFLUENCE AND IT WILL ANSWER HIS MAJESTY'S WORRY ABOUT **WHO IS BEHIND** THE UNREST! HE **DISTRUSTS** JEWS...IT'LL BE EASY...

IN 1987 A JAPANESE LANGUAGE EDITION OF THE "PROTOCOLS" APPEARED IN **JAPAN!**

これからの10年間　矢島鈞次
ユダヤ・プロトコール
超裏読み術　あなたにも起こるショッキングな!
なぜ愚かなのか...この恐るべき真実!!

IN 1988 THE PALESTINIAN ACTIVIST GROUP **HAMAS** PUBLISHED THE "PROTOCOLS" TO DENOUNCE ZIONISTS.

بروتوكولات حكماء صهيون

AND IN 1990, **THIS** APPEARED IN **DAMASCUS!**

SET THEM SIDE BY SIDE, GRAVES, AND YOU WILL SEE **OBVIOUS PLAGIARISM** OF JOLY'S "DIALOGUE"!

I SEE...BE PATIENT WHILE I GO THROUGH IT...YES! YES! YES!

DIALOGUE IN HELL

FIRST DIALOGUE

Machiavelli: The evil instinct in man is more powerful than the good. Man leans more toward the evil than the good; fear and power have more control over him than reason.... All men seek power, and there is none who would not be an oppressor if he could; all, or nearly all, are ready to sacrifice the rights of others to their own interests.

What restrains these ravenous animals that we call men? In the beginnings of society, it is brute force, without control; later, it is the law, that is, force again, ruled by certain forms. You have consulted all the sources of history; everywhere force appears before justice.

Political liberty is only a relative idea....

PROTOCOLS

NUMBER 1, paras. 3-6

It must be noted that men with bad instincts are more in number than the good, and therefore the best results in governing them are attained by violence and terrorization, and not by academic discussions. Every man aims at power, everyone would like to become a dictator if only he could, and rare indeed are the men who would not be willing to sacrifice the welfare of all for the sake of securing their own welfare. What has restrained the beasts of prey who are called men? What has served for their guidance hitherto?

In the beginnings of the structure of society they were subjected to brute and blind force: afterwards to law, which is the same force, only disguised. I draw the conclusion that by the law of nature right lies in force. Political freedom is an idea but not a fact.

▶▲ Will Eisner uses more than his fair share of conjecture when he re-enacts the times in which the original Protocols were created, in Tsarist Russia. This is done to give known facts a human, believable element—something Eisner was a master at.

▶▲ At the very end of the book, Eisner shows how *The Protocols of the Elders of Zion* is still being published today, despite the fact that it has been proved a fraud several times over.

▶ In a large section of his book, Eisner has two people compare the alleged Protocols and the book that most scholars have concluded was the basis for it.

▼ The superheroes of *The 99* live and act in a world similar to ours, where they are public heroes. Published both in Arabic and English and sold all over the world, the style of these comics is exactly like that of superhero comics from the U.S., as can be seen here.

◄ A page from the origin-issue of *The 99*, i.e. the story that gives the background to the universe in which the comics take place. Here we see how the librarians from the invaded Baghdad immerse ninety-nine jewels into the Tigris River, in order to soak up all the wisdom contained in the ink that was spilled as the books of Baghdad were thrown in.

▲ A pivotal moment in *The 99* at the beginning of the first issue. The sentiment spoken by this character is shared by the comics' creator Al-Mutawa, who has set out to change the world with his comics.

The 99 Virtues of Allah

The Koran says that God has ninety-nine names. Each name is also a virtue, and among them are strength, courage, wisdom, and justice. A good Muslim should strive to let these characteristics guide his or her life, but human beings are imperfect and each person only has a handful of these traits. Only Allah can have all ninety-nine. These characteristics are the basis for *The 99*, the world's first superhero comic book directly inspired by Muslim culture and faith.

The comics were created by Dr. Naif Al-Mutawa and the story begins with a pivotal moment in Islamic history—the 1258 Mongol invasion of Baghdad, which left the city in ruins and led to the dumping of books from its famed library into the Tigris River. The legend has it that the ink turned the waters black, and in this story some librarians escape and are able to place ninety-nine special stones in the river to soak up the wisdom otherwise lost. Eight hundred years later, the mysterious stones are found in different corners of the world by, more or less, ordinary people from ninety-nine different countries, who are then turned into superheroes. None of the heroes pray or read the Koran. Some of them are Muslims, others not, since Al-Mutawa thought that the ninety-nine properties are universal and belong to humanity. Among the heroes we find the classic, strong, Hulk-like character Jabbar and the more original Hadya, whose ability is to always find the right path in life. The characters are roughly divided between men and women and only a few of the women wear the Islamic headscarf.

The great conflict in the story is between two different groups of the ninety-nine recruits, groups that have different goals. This is used as a metaphor for what is happening in the Muslim world today, where different groups use religion to achieve their various objectives. Also, all obstacles that the ninety-nine superheroes encounter must be overcome by the combined power of at least three or more of them. Through this, Al-Mutawa promotes the values of cooperation and unity in the Muslim world.

Although the comic has its roots in Islam, there is no direct allusion to religion in the stories. This is to strengthen the feeling that it deals with universal values. But even if the comic is not religious, Al-Mutawa wants it to communicate Islamic virtues to the reader, like generosity, strength, wisdom, or foresight.

Al-Mutawa is a Kuwaiti businessman who has taken an American institution and given it an Arabic makeover. Like Al-Mutawa himself, who spent his childhood summers at camps in New Hampshire, *The 99* is a mixture of East and West. The form is American, and the creative team is full of American veterans from the superhero genre. In order to be successful, the company has chosen to work with renowned artists and writers like Fabian Nicieza, Stuart Moore, Dan Panosian, John McCrea, and Sean Parsons—all of whom have worked with both Marvel and DC Comics. But the core of the comic is Muslim. By making use of the history, culture, and traditions of the Middle East, Al-Mutawa wants to create positive and inspiring role models that will also appeal to children outside this part of the world.

◀ Art from one of the covers of *The 99*. The superheroes of *The 99* must always work together to be able to achieve their goals, symbolizing the need for people in the Arab world to work together to solve problems.

A part of a triptych depicting the scenes from the Sino-Japanese War of 1894–1895. Here we see *The Great Battle of Ansong Ford: The Valor of Captain Matsusaki.* The theatrical stance of the soldiers and

Chapter 2

War!
What is it Good For?

War Brings Out the Best in People

War, comics, and propaganda make for a fruitful combination. The basic setup of war, with two protagonists who naturally have opposing views, lends itself to stories that are filled with emotions, opinions, and outright propaganda. The comics are often produced by cartoonists belonging to either party in the war, and naturally show things from their subjective viewpoint. Sometimes openly, sometimes you have to look for it, but there is almost always a bias.

There are many ways in which war can be featured in comics: war can be part of another genre, such as superhero, fantasy, or historical stories; war can be used as the setting for dramatic storylines about the fate of people in dreadful times; war can be used to make a political point; and then there is the genre of war comics itself, where there have been two major producers of war titles: America and Great Britain.

In America, comics based soley on stories about war were introduced soon after the invention of the comic book format, in the late 1930s. During World War II, patriotism flared and most comics with themes of war—which were not restricted to actual war comics—depicted American soldiers as heroic, superior, and victorious, and the enemy as unheroic cowards, often even as almost sub-human. This, of course, is only natural given the circumstances, but doesn't make them any less propagandistic when viewed today.

During WWII, the superhero genre was also quite new, and was used extensively as a tool of propaganda. The charge was led by Superman and Captain America, and these colorful spandex-clad figures did exactly what their readers wished they could do: they flew through the enemy lines, and more often than not, actually gave Hitler a punch on the nose. Talk about wish fulfilment, as well as overt propaganda.

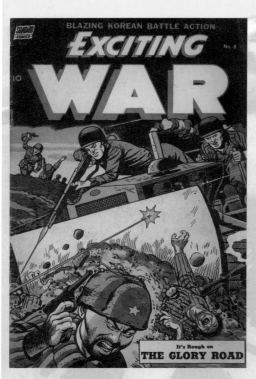

◄◄ Early on, creators of comics adapted to the feelings of the people and depicted American soldiers and superheroes battling the enemy. Here Captain Marvel and Bulletman face off against Hitler's very own superhero, Captain Nazi (no prize for guessing who was victorious in this battle).

◄ Issue #8 of *Exciting War*, with the evocative subtitle *Blazing Korean Battle Action*, from 1953. It contains, among other things, stories drawn by the master draftsman Alex Toth. Notice the Communist Koreans (so designated by the red star on the hats) being bulldozed by the brave American soldiers.

► The first issue of the American comic book *The 'Nam* from 1986. Written by Vietnam veteran Doug Murray, this relatively recent war comic told the story of a ficticious American soldier fighting in the war. The story progressed one month per issue, thus having the comic always staying in the same relative time to the events depicted.

►► Cover to the British comic book *Air Ace Picture Library* from 1962, with art by Pino Dell'Orco. *Air Ace* contained, as the title indicates, stories about war in the skies. This one shows a German airborne soldier reconsidering the things he does in the line of duty.

Background illustration An issue of *Battle Picture Library* from 1966, with a painted cover by the prolific cover artist Jordi Penalva. The British war comics were often pretty realistic, and did not contain depictions of the enemy as sub-humans.

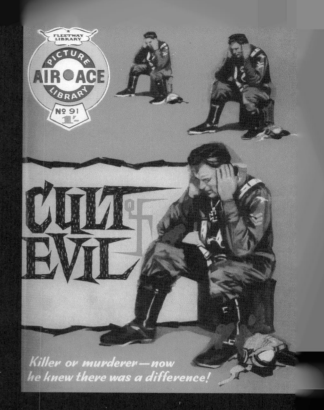

WWII holds a special allure in war comics, and there are still comics published today that are set during that period. Other "popular" wars in American war comics were the Korean War and the Vietnam War. There have been comics about other conflicts, but never on such a scale. During the Korean War, for example, EC Comics was at its peak and produced titles like *Two-Fisted Tales* and *Frontline Combat*, which contained some of the best war comics ever, often actually anti-war in theme.

A special mention should go to the Marvel comic *G.I. Joe: A Real American Hero*, which debuted in the 1980s. This was a comic based on a series of action figures and focused on a fictional counter-terrorist team in a contemporary setting. The comics were actually often very well written by the scriptwriter Larry Hama, but the title of this series says it all...

In Great Britain, the business of war comics was huge in the 1950s and 1960s, and then slowly withered away during the 1970s. War comics were mostly published as small black-and-white comic books, with titles like *War*, *Battle*, *Air Ace*, and *War at Sea*. The genre got started in the latter part of the 1950s and was soon dominating the British comics market with dozens upon dozens of titles, many of which published weekly. The comics were mostly written by British scriptwriters, many having served in WWII, but most of the cartoonists drawing the comics were from Italy and Spain. The stories were often more realistic than their American counterparts, both in the drawing style of the comics and the storylines, but still inevitably showed how the "good guys" (the British, the Americans, and the Australians) won over the "bad guys" (often referred to as "Krauts," "Jerries," "Japs," and "Eyeties").

In France and Belgium, World War I, or the Great War, is more often featured than in the American/British arena, with the great Jaques Tardi as the main cartoonist keeping the memory of this war alive with titles like *C'était la Guerre des Tranchées* (*It Was the War of the Trenches*) and *Varlot soldat* (*The Soldier Varlot*). Today, the genre of war comics is not big anywhere in the world. However, comics about war in its various forms are still used quite a lot, as will be shown in this chapter.

▲ The second, and final, page of the comic made directly for the magazine *Look*. Here both Hitler and Stalin are defeated and brought to justice, a wish shared by a lot of people in the world in 1940, not least by the persecuted groups of people in Germany and Russia.

▲▲ The "hate-article" in the SS magazine *Der Schwartze Korps* (*The Black Corps*) from 1940, which describes Jerry Siegel in very anti-Semitic ways.

▲ Just before the end of the war, Siegel and Shuster took another stab at the Nazis through their character Superman. Here is a page from *Overseas Comics* #44 from 1945, which was produced for the American military in Europe and distributed by the Special Services A.S.F. of the U.S. Army.

Superman Ends World War II

The character Superman was created during the 1930s by two young Jewish men, Jacob "Jerry" Siegel and Joseph "Joe" Shuster. Superman debuted in the comic book *Action Comics* in 1938. Faster than a speeding bullet, Superman became a huge success, and Siegel and Shuster realized that they had a megaphone with which they could talk to large numbers of people.

In 1940 they did just that. In a two-page story for the magazine *Look*, they showed how they would want things to be in the world. The comic was called *How Superman Would End the War*. On the first page we see how Superman races to the Siegfried line—the defensive line that the Germans had built against France—destroys the cannons, rips the covers off the concrete fortifications, and invites the French forces to "Come and get 'em!" On the second page, the story becomes really interesting. Here Super-man continues into Germany and captures Hitler, then flies on to Moscow and grabs Joseph "Joe" Stalin to deliver them both to the League of Nations in Geneva. The League of Nations was the organization started after World War I that ultimately failed to prevent World War II from breaking out, and later was replaced by the United Nations. Why Italy's Mussolini or Japan's Hirohito were spared I do not know, but the explanation for Stalin's inclusion was that Russia had not yet become an ally of the U.S. at the time.

The fact that Siegel and Shuster were aware of what Hitler was doing to Jews is indicated by the line that Superman delivers to Hitler while holding him aloft in one hand: "I'd like to land a strictly non-Aryan sock on your jaw." This also reveals how the two Jewish creators viewed their character. Superman isn't exactly your archetypal Aryan stereotype with blond hair, and it is quite evident that Siegel and Shuster saw him as an extension of themselves. There are several other extraordinary facts about this comic. One is that it was published in February 1940, almost two years before the attack on Pearl Harbor, which prompted the U.S. to enter the war. In 1940, most Americans were still not particularly interested in the conflict.

Another interesting fact is that the comic was actually noticed and commented upon in Germany. A large hate-article was published in the weekly newspaper of the SS, *Das Schwarze Korps*, in 1940, in which almost the whole comic was reprinted and Jerry Siegel was attacked viciously, called "an intellectually and physically circumcised chap" and "The inventive Israelite," among other derogatory remarks. The article ended with the following sentence: Jerry "Siegellack stinks. Woe to the American youth, who must live in such a poisoned atmosphere and don't even notice the poison they swallow daily."

Joe Shuster is not mentioned in the article. The writer probably thought that they could safely ascertain the Jewish ancestry of Jerry Siegel from his family name, but could not do the same with Shuster.

One can also add the urban legend that Joseph Goebbels himself, the Nazi minister for propaganda, publicly denounced Superman in the middle of a Reichtag meeting, furiously announcing: "Superman is a Jew." This has been repeated again and again, but I have yet to see any tangible evidence that it really happened. What is known, however, is that Goebbels read a lot of foreign media and sent caricatures of Hitler to the Führer himself, who was mightily amused. So he might have seen himself being swept away by the Man of Steel.

There were many stories of superheroes taking part in the war effort, but none as direct in their message of how things should be and what superheroes, if they existed, should do about the war.

Punching Hitler on the Nose

Following hot on the heels of the success of Superman, a whole genre of muscle-bound heroes emerged. The "Golden Age" of this genre coincided with World War II, and subsequently superhero comics were enlisted and used as tools of propaganda.

In fact, it was not only the superheroes; practically all heroes in American comics were used to attack the enemies, and especially the Nazis, in one way or another. Superheroes were particularly suited for this, though. It is probably not too much of an assumption to think that the image of a person who voluntarily gives up his ordinary life to don a uniform and battle bad guys resonated well with a nation at war.

All kinds of superheroes were pictured fighting the Nazis, clobbering fictitious and fictionalized versions of the enemy. Indeed no superhero was worth his salt if he wasn't prepared to engage in battle with the Japanese and the Germans on a regular basis. One of the best-remembered is Joe Simon and Jack Kirby's Captain America fighting Adolf Hitler himself, giving him a big wallop on the cover of Cap's very first issue. But he was far from alone. The Sub-Mariner, for instance, written by the young Bill Everett, attacked Nazi submarines on a regular basis, and the Human Torch, under the guidance of writer Carl Burgos, burned big holes in the plans of both domestic and German Nazis. Often the heroes were created for the sole purpose of fighting America's enemies, and were as forgettable as their stories. A more potent character was Uncle Sam, who was frequently used as an iconic figure in these stories, often fighting alongside other superheroes in the battle against the enemy.

Looking through the covers of superhero comics from the war years, it is evident how much they resemble official propaganda posters from that era. The same rhetorical techniques and strategies were used in order to attract readers. The ideas represented in the U.S. superhero comics were simple, often supporting the myths of American superiority and the enemy's inferiority, and depicting imminent victory. The official doctrine of

President Franklin D. Roosevelt was that the makers of popular culture should contribute with a form of propaganda that informed rather than inflamed. But comics writers were soon responding to the angry mood of the American people, and comic books became more hate-filled, depicting the representatives of the Axis as stereotypical villains and the American troops as equally stereotypical heroes.

The comic book industry was actually able to boost its sales during WWII, because the help in the war effort meant that comic books were spared from paper recycling. Sales tripled from 1940 to 1945. The clearest sign of how intimately linked the first flowering of the superhero genre and the war propaganda was is the fact that as soon as WWII ended, public interest in these comics subsided and sales dropped like a stone. The genre has survived, and made several comebacks, but it is not surprising that this first period of superhero comics is called the Golden Age, as there has never been such a perfect enemy as the Nazis to fight.

◄ Captain America, probably the most potent of all the comics symbols of America, but also a character created by two Jewish cartoonists, Joe Simon and Jack Kirby (born Jacob Kurtzberg). It's not surprising that the cover of the very first issue of *Captain America*, from 1940 (even though it says March 1941 on the cover), had the image of the hero beating up Hitler. Remember that this was long before Pearl Harbor, at a time when the U.S. was not involved in the war.

Background illustration In the aptly titled *Star Spangled Comics*, the superhero the Guardian, assisted by "the Newsboy Legion" (clearly created for the average readers of the comic to identify with), took part in the war and kicked some Japs. The comics were made by Joe Simon and Jack Kirby.

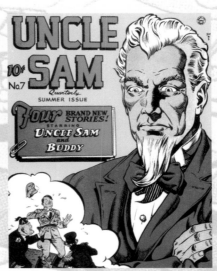

◄ The iconic figure of Uncle Sam was used extensively during the war years, not least in superhero comics. Here he is seen as a larger than life figure, looming high above Hitler, Mussolini, and Tojo, with the demeanor and appearance of a school-master reprimanding his naughty "children."

▲ The animation business also got into the war effort. This is the poster for the animated Donald Duck short *Der Fuehrer's Face*, an Academy Award-winning film from Walt Disney.

► One of the most striking covers from the war years, starring Hitler. A pretty strange cover, with Hitler based on a photo, and several superheroes attacking him at once but not really making any difference. This issue is from 1941, with art by Bob Wood and Charles Biro.

The Beast is Dead!

A singular comic, unique in every way, was produced during the occupation of France in World War II and published just months after the liberation. It retells the history of the war in the form of a satirical anthropomorphic comic. This comic is well-known in the French-speaking parts of the world, but sadly has never become as famous in the English-speaking territories.

La bête est morte! (*The Beast Is Dead!*)—also known as *La Guerre Mondiale chez les Animaux* (*World War II Among the Animals*)—was based on texts written by Victor Dancette and Jacques Zimmermann, and illustrated by Edmond-François Calvo, during the occupation. It was published as two volumes in 1944 and 1945 respectively. The story is an allegory and begins with young squirrels asking their grandfather how he lost his leg. What he tells them is the whole story of WWII, with the animals representing different

nationalities, just as in Art Spiegelman's masterpiece *Maus*. The Germans are barbarian wolves, with Hitler as the Great Wolf himself, and the French are carefree rabbits, but also other rodents and frogs—even though the very elongated General de Gaulle is a great stork. The British are fierce bulldogs, the Americans are efficient buffaloes, the Italians are wolf-clad hyenas, the Russians are polar bears, and the Japanese are yellow monkeys.

The design of the character of Hitler greatly resembles that which Tex Avery used in his animated short *Blitz Wolf* from 1942, but it's doubtful that Calvo would have had an opportunity to see it. More likely, Calvo was inspired by the ancient traditions of telling fables using animals as iconic stand-ins for people, a tradition that had been rejuvenated by the animators at the Walt Disney Studio in the twentieth century. Calvo has been

▶ In Calvo's story, Adolf Hitler became the Great Wolf, Hermann Göring was the decorated pig, and Joseph Goebbels was the talkative polecat. In particular the image of Hitler as a wolf stuck in the minds of many, and has been used time and time again in caricatures.

▼ This is the scene that refers to the Holocaust. Mothers are separated from their children, and Jews are put up against the wall and executed. Pretty heavy stuff, considering that this was aimed at children. Or was it?

4. « *Poursuivant plus particulièrement leur vengeance contre certaines tribus d'animaux pacifiques que nous hébergions et à qui nous avions bien souvent ouvert nos portes pour les abriter contre la fureur de la Bête déchaînée, les hordes du Grand Loup avaient commencé le plus atroce des plans de destruction des races rebelles, dispersant les membres de leurs tribus dans des régions lointaines, séparant les femmes de leurs époux, les enfants de leurs mères, visant ainsi l'anéantissement total de ces foules inoffensives qui n'avaient commis d'autre crime que celui de ne pas se soumettre à la volonté de la Bête.*

5. « *Bientôt d'ailleurs, nous ne pûmes supporter le joug répugnant de ces Barbares, et notre hostilité, pour ne pas être officielle n'en devint pas moins totale. Mais ils multipliaient leurs espions et tendaient partout des pièges pour nous prendre en défaut. Par représailles, des milliers d'entre nous furent emmenés en captivité, maltraités et soumis aux plus durs et aux plus rebutants travaux. Des milliers d'autres ont payé de leur vie le fait de ne pas vouloir courber l'échine devant l'envahisseur. Quand les mauvais traitements ne les tuaient pas assez vite, de féroces massacres venaient rayer des contrôles les plus irréductibles de chez nous. Leur souvenir doit rester impérissable parmi nous.*

C'est

ce que vous pourrez voir dans notre

deuxième fascicule :

la bête est terrassée

—CALVO—

▲ **A stunning full page by Calvo, depicting the French resistance finally throwing the barbarous wolves out of Paris. It is a pastiche of the French painter Eugène Delacroix and his famous painting *Liberty Leading the People*, inspired by the Paris uprising of 1830, in itself a powerful work of propaganda.**

called the French Walt Disney, and Disney did sue him for the design of the wolf's snouts, which had to be changed.

The story in *La bête est morte!* is very graphic, in every sense of the word. Not only are the drawings by Calvo beautiful, but the depictions of war are sometimes excruciating, considering that this was aimed mostly at young readers. The animals in the story are maimed, killed, tortured, and persecuted. It is a fable and good does win over evil, but on the way some really monstrous acts are committed. Due to the fact that it was produced during and just after all of these things were happening in Europe, it is not hard to see that Calvo wanted it that way. The use of a style that causes the reader to think of cute and cuddly children's stories also makes the atrocities committed in the story that much more effective upon the reader.

It has been said that *La bête est morte!* contains the very first mention of the Holocaust in comics. The mention is short and vague, but information was scarce at the time. The first comic to mention the Holocaust is often said to be *Master Race* by the American Bernie Krigstein from 1955, and the first official mention in a French comic was in 1984. The "beast" in the title, of course, refers to Hitler, but at the time of publication his death was still wishful thinking. No matter what, *La bête est morte!* is a powerful story and, just as it set out to do, has influenced generations of readers and given them iconic images with which to make what happened during WWII understandable. The force of the story is still evident today, as it is only now about to be turned into a full-length animated movie.

▼▼ Norakuro was the most famous of the Japanese comics characters of the period before WWII. The character was a stray dog who soon joined the Japanese army (also depicted as dogs) to fight the Chinese (who were all pigs). A very popular children's comic, chock-full of propaganda.

▼ *The Great Victory of Our Troops Near Asan*, part of the triptych about the Sino-Japanese War in 1894–1895. Here we can see how the Chinese were slaughtered by the Japanese soldiers, who were equipped with modern firing weapons. Notice that, in this terrible slaughter, almost no blood is shown, befitting the sense of it all taking place in a theme park version of reality.

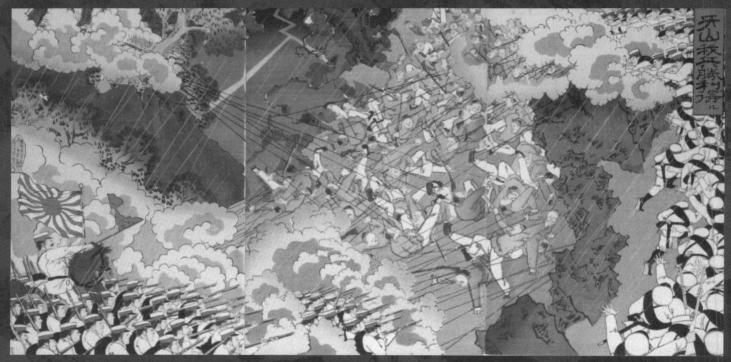

Japan at War

In Japan, storytelling with pictures is an ancient art form. Many traits of modern comics can be found dating as far back as the eleventh century. These stories have often been used in the service of propaganda, especially so in times of war. After the opening of Japan to the world and the subsequent Meiji Restoration in the second half of the nineteenth century, Japan grew into a major force in Asia and partook in several wars. Most of them have made their marks on popular culture.

The First Sino-Japanese War was fought during 1894 and 1895 between Japan and China over the control of Korea. China was defeated and humiliated, since Japan had modernized its army with European help and assistance. The Japanese army was modeled after European armies and was devastatingly superior to the Chinese, who still fought with traditional swords. During this period, the preferred way of communicating with images was with woodblock prints, which depicted scenes from the war in very nationalistic ways, printed sequentially as long triptychs. These pretty obvious wartime propaganda efforts were very colorful and very theatrical, making it look like the war took place in some kind of weird theme park. It is evident that they were intended as tools of propaganda, even for readers outside of China, as there were sometimes captions with explanations in European languages.

The Russo-Japanese War in 1904–05 was fought between Japan and Russia, again over Korea but also over Manchuria, as both empires had ambitions to expand their influence in the same area. Japan defeated Russia, making this the first time an Asian country defeated a Western country in modern times.

This was one of many wars to leave its mark on popular culture. At the time, the Western— especially the British and American—way of making comics had entered Japan, and influenced how stories were told with pictures. The youth magazine *Yônen no tomo* (*The Children's Friend*), from the first decade of the twentieth century, contained some of the earliest comics that look like modern day manga. The magazine also contained illustrated reports on the progress of the war in 1905, which were aimed at a young Japanese audience.

The 1930s, when the entire country of Japan was preparing for new military confrontations, was a time of mounting nationalism, something that didn't go unnoticed in popular culture. Japanese comics had evolved even further under the influence of the imported and translated American comic strips. One of the most successful of the Japanese comics of this era was *Norakuro*, by Suiho Tagawa, a story about a stray dog in an anthropomorphic version of Japan. This children's manga started out as a fairly normal comic for young readers, but soon tuned in with the militaristic, nationalistic sensibility of Japan and had the main character join the army and fight the Chinese (depicted as pigs). For the most part of its existence, the comics about Norakuro dealt with war, but always in a children's fashion, without showing any blood. *Norakuro* was only one of many children's manga from this period with themes of war and patriotism.

Since the country's surrender at the end of World War II, Japan has only been allowed to have "Self-Defense Forces." Because the U.S. needed a strong ally in this part of the world, this self-defense force was allowed to grow and is today the sixth largest army in the world, but has never really actively been part of a war again. Thus far the Japanese army have only taken part in peace-keeping missions with the UN or assisted the U.S. in Iraq, and this has not generated nearly as much propaganda within comics as in the days before and during WWII.

◄ **A spread from a Japanese children's comic from the 1930s. Children's comics of this era were filled with war-themed stories. This example shows a comic that was built around the fairly new technology of tanks, making these war machines out to be almost mythical characters in themselves and war to be a funny and interesting adventure.**

Nazi War Propaganda for Boys

▶ **The cover of a collection of *Picture Stories From the War*. The cover was the same throughout most of the war, with the content being changed as new comics were produced.**

During the Nazi regime in Germany, the import of American comics was stopped, and German kids had to turn to other sources for their reading entertainment. One of those available was *Bilderbogen vom Kriege* (*Picture Stories from the War*), which offered the young readers some interesting stories to devour.

These comics were an odd combination of old and new. They consisted of pictures in boxes arranged on a page with rhyming text below, which at the time was a form that made the comics feel like they were from the nineteenth century. No speech balloons, onomatopoetic words, or any other modern comics inventions were used. The images, on the other hand, were in full color, painted, and very much in the style of the times.

According to the covers of the collections of these comics, they were made by an old publisher of picture stories, but in reality they were produced by Deutschen Propaganda-Atelier (The Propaganda Atelier of Germany), a subdivision of the more famous Reichsministerium für Volksaufklärung und Propaganda (Ministry of Public Enlightenment and Propaganda). This was, of course, the department

of propaganda in Germany—the world's most powerful propaganda machine during WWII.

The aim of these comics was stated clearly in the foreword of the collections: "*Bilderbogen vom Kriege* are aimed at all German-speaking people, both small and big, young and old, with the demand to in their own way do right by the German soldiers' heroic spirit and keep the memory of their deeds alive for children and grandchildren." But their aim was not at all as magnanimous as this might sound.

Bilderbogen vom Kriege were aimed at a young, male audience, and one should remember that at this time most young boys in Germany were part of the Hitlerjugend, a paramilitary training system, where everyone's goal was the elevation to soldier. In Hitlerjugend, the myth of the hero was cultivated vigorously. Most of these comics, therefore, told the stories of brave deeds done by private soldiers; soldiers that had done more than could be expected in the line of duty. There were also a fair number of comics reassuring the reader of the supremacy of the German military, with titles like *Deutschland beherrscht die See* (*Germany Rules the Sea*).

The war was shown as a clean and exciting adventure, where a young man could make a name for himself through bravery. There are many exploding planes, sunken ships, etc., but almost never any dead bodies, blood, or anything of the like. The enemy was also mostly treated with respect and never shown as the evil sub-humans that wartime propaganda tends to gravitate towards, most likely out of the rationale that it is more honorable to beat a brave enemy.

There were about eighty of these one-pagers made, up until 1943, when the turning of the war made them less of a priority. Today they give us a glimpse of another world: a world where young boys were expected to believe that war was an exciting adventure in which valor and camaraderie were cherished, and Germany was about to conquer the globe.

▼ One of the more historically accurate comics from *Bilderbogen vom Kriege*. It tells the story of the German conquest of Holland, and ends with an ominous image and text, in rhyme, that tells the reader, "Whoever allies with the English, finds death through Germany's military."

Kampf um Rotterdam

Stabsfeldwebel Hübner

◄ This is an example of the heroic stories that *Bilderbogen vom Kriege* were full of. Here we see how the soldier Hübner lands his aircraft, despite injuries. Also, notice how the enemy is shown as traditional soldiers, even though the text ends with a comment on the fact that the soldiers of Holland soon would get what was coming to them.

◄ An example of one of the later episodes of *Bilderbogen vom Kriege*, where the heroic German Luftwaffe chases away the British airplanes bombing German soil. The war was coming closer, and after this production of these comics ceased.

Background illustration A German propaganda comic, which was dropped behind the frontline during the offensive against Russia in 1940. Here we see that Russian soldiers surrendering will be offered cigarettes and food and be treated gently by the German soldiers.

Getting Undressed for the War

War is, by definition, a very male phenomenon. Not getting into the discussion of whether the world might have been a better and more peaceful place if women had ruled, war is traditionally started by men and fought between men, with women being affected by the war as civilian casualties, losing family members, and/or being raped, pillaged, looted, starved, and so on. So it follows that propaganda comics sent to the predominantly male troops were often very male-oriented, not to mention chauvinistic and sexist.

During World War II, this was probably best exemplified by the British comic strip *Jane*, by Norman Pett. *Jane's Journal—The Diary of a Bright Young Thing* began as a strip in the British newspaper the *Daily Mirror* in 1932, but it was during WWII that it became a truly national phenomenon, and was seen as boosting the morale of the men in military service.

Jane, or Jane Gay (a play on the name Lady Jane Grey), was a hapless young woman who got into one adventure after another, never missing a chance to lose her clothes. Or rather, the cartoonist never missed a chance to let Jane's clothes be ripped off, burned off, eaten by insects, or removed in any other weird way he could envision to have her at least appear in her underwear every third strip or so.

◀ Part of the famous strip where Jane showed herself fully naked for the first time, and supposedly sent the British troops onward five miles in just one day at the front in North Africa.

◀◀ A large compilation of all the war strips with *Jane* was published as late as the 1970s. This is an interesting read, starting with the enlisting of Jane's male friends, and ending with her returning to have a summer vacation after the war is over, tanning on the beach next to an undetonated mine.

The best myth about the comic strip *Jane* is also connected to her habit of inadvertently undressing at all times. The cartoonist Pett always kept Jane's stripping in the comic strip on the level, never letting her get totally naked, even though he was frequently asked to do so. When he finally gave in and, in 1943, drew a strip where Jane accidently (it's always accidental in *Jane* . . .) falls into the middle of a bunch of British soldiers while getting out of a bath, fully naked, it is said that the British Army advanced five miles in North Africa.

And then there was Milton Caniff's beautiful strip *Male Call*, which he made on a voluntary basis between 1943 and 1946. Caniff was drafted, twice, but both times rejected on account of his health. Feeling not a little bit frustrated and guilty about this, he volunteered to create a strip for free, to be distributed through military newspapers. At the end of the war, this meant that 3,000 papers carried *Male Call*, making it the most well-distributed comic strip ever.

Male Call is a gag-a-day strip featuring the beautiful woman Miss Lace, who seems to live close to an American military base and always hangs out with the enlisted men. Never choosing any of them, she is presented as the perpetual maybe—and more than a lingering thought in many of the readers' minds.

Neither *Jane* nor *Male Call* contained much overt political propaganda, but reading them today it is very clear that they were produced during a conflict, which makes the need to draw clear lines between "us" and "them" so much more urgent. These comic strips show the world from a very specific, Western viewpoint—a viewpoint from which there is no doubt as to the outcome of the war, or for that matter who has the strongest and most potent military might. How's that for propaganda?

▼ Miss Lace of *Male Call*, by Milton Caniff. She was a walking, talking pin-up girl, designed so that her mere presence in the strip was enough to satisfy millions of male readers in the military service during WWII. From the collection of Caj Byqvist.

◄▼ In *Male Call*, part of the morale-boosting was due to Miss Lace always addressing enlisted men as "General," and often treating them better than the actual officers. She was also always going out with different men, but never ending up in love with anyone. The promise of a maybe was what every soldier lived for. From the collection of Caj Byqvist.

Barefoot Gen:
A Transnational Peace Project

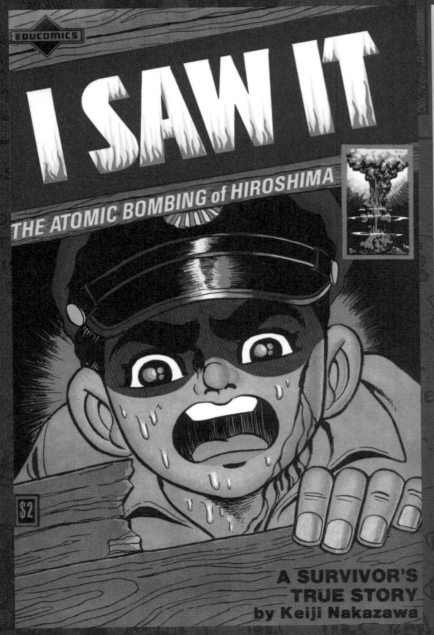

◄ The first, short version of Nakazawa's experiences was published in English as *I Saw It* in 1982. It contains the most grueling parts of the bombing, with a framework story about how Nakazawa worked to become a professional cartoonist in order to tell his story to the world.

▲ This is the scene that Nakazawa saw when he awoke after the initial blast from the atom bombing of Hiroshima. Taken from the short version of *I Saw It*, which was published in color in the English edition.

▶ Nakazawa describes the period after the bombing in a way that almost nobody else has dared do in popular culture. To say that you are affected as a reader is an understatement. Powerful anti-bomb propaganda, indeed.

There has never been a more grueling war comic than the autobiographical *Hadashi no Gen*, or *Barefoot Gen*, as it is called in English. This comic was published in a boys' magazine in Japan in the early 1970s and has been spread across the world in an effort to raise awareness of the human suffering caused by atomic weapons.

The cartoonist Keiji Nakazawa was six years old when the Americans dropped an atomic bomb on Hiroshima. Despite being just about a half a mile from the epicenter, Nakazawa survived, but only to see his family die in the fires that followed the bombing, and experience first-hand how people melted in the streets and filled the few remaining open waters in the city in an effort to stop the agonizing pain from radiation burns. Later on he would witness how people slowly died from radiation, killed each other over the few remaining scraps of food, and so on. *Barefoot Gen* is a heart-wrenching story, but at the same time it contains a positive quality personified in the character Gen, who may despair from time to time but never gives up and always tries to keep his spirits up, no matter what.

Nakazawa first told his story in a short, forty-five-page long comic called *Oré wa mita* (*I Saw It*) in 1972. When his editor urged him to create a longer

piece, he embarked on the journey that would result in a collected story of ten 200-page long volumes, encompassing not only the bombing of Hiroshima, but life before in the war-ridden, patriotic Japan, as well as the subsequent life of Gen into the 1950s and the time of the American occupation. It is evident when reading *Barefoot Gen* that Nakazawa is against the use of atomic weapons, but also that he strongly condemns militarism, and clearly blames not only the Americans but also the Japanese military for what happened.

The theme of *Barefoot Gen* had (and still has) a universal appeal, and soon a wholly unique phenomenon within comics occurred: Project Gen. It all started in 1976 when Japanese peace activists Masahiro Oshima and Yukio Aki walked across America as part of that year's Transcontinental Walk for Peace and Social Justice. With them, they brought a copy of *Hadashi no Gen*, which shocked and affected their fellow American walkers. Back in Japan, they contacted Nakazawa and founded Project Gen, a non-profit, all-volunteer group of young Japanese and Americans living in Japan, and went on to translate the first four volumes of *Gen* into English. This also resulted in volumes translated and published in French, German, Italian, Portuguese, Swedish, Norwegian, Indonesian, Tagalog, and Esperanto. In many countries, this was the first Japanese comic to be published, long before "manga" became a household word.

Recently Project Gen has been revived; a new team of volunteers has translated all ten volumes of *Barefoot Gen*, and right now they are being published in various languages across the world. A separate group has made sure that all ten volumes have been published in Russian, the other major nuclear power in the world.

Namie Asazuma, the current coordinator of Project Gen, expresses the wishes of a group like this in an afterword to the English editions: "In the hope that humanity will never repeat the terrible tragedy of the atomic bombing, the volunteers of Project Gen want children and adults all over the world to hear Gen's story. Through translations like this one, we want to help Gen speak to people in different countries in their own languages. Our prayer is that *Barefoot Gen* will contribute in some small way to the abolition of nuclear weapons before this new century is over."

Marvel at the Support of the Iraq War

There seems to be an intimate link between superheroes and war. As I have stated earlier, there is something about (albeit fictitious) characters who don battle gear and fight the just fight against evil that resonates with a people at war. Since superhero comics is a genre that almost only exists in the U.S., this means that superheroes are inevitably enlisted in most modern American wars.

The most recent example of this phenomenon can be found in a series of comic books made especially by Marvel Comics to support the American troops in the Iraq War, and promote good will towards the U.S. military in general. Since 2005, six issues have been produced and more than one million copies donated by Marvel, most of which have been sent to American soldiers abroad, but also handed out to families at home, and sold at special stores across the world. The comics feature the superhero group the New Avengers, a collection of Marvel characters led by the most iconic, patriotic superhero of them all: Captain America.

These comic books are propaganda through and through, and as such very interesting to read. And it is not a kind of sneaky, backdoor propaganda that is used. Right out on the cover it states: "Marvel salutes the real heroes, the men and women of the U.S. military." The cover also sports the logo for America Supports You, a division of the American Department of Defense with the aim to raise support for the American troops.

The enemies in these stories are almost always the usual adversaries of superheroes, i.e., mad scientists, armies of robots, the would-be world dominating group Hydra, and so on. The superheroes are not sent in to attack the real enemies of the American soldiers, as was done in superhero comics during World War II—probably because times have changed and readers would not buy that anymore. There is also almost never any blood or real causalities. War is shown as a clean and neat battle between good and evil.

One example of how these comics work is an issue called *Letters Home*, which tells the story of how a satellite used to send the American soldiers' e-mail home is kidnapped by the aforementioned group Hydra. Captain America, the Silver Surfer, Ghost Rider, and the Punisher are sent in, and during their fights with members of Hydra (all clad in green bodysuits that make them look alike and therefore not really human), we can read letters that the human alter egos of these superheroes write home. A powerful allegory, and very well written by Stuart Moore.

This is not the first time Marvel produced comics in support of the American forces. In 2005, writer Chuck Austen and artists Ben Lai and Ray Lai made the comic book *Guard Force: The Army National Guard*. This comic is not about superheroes, but tells the story of Americans who are part of the Army National Guard, and the stories are told to show that these are just ordinary citizens, doing their duty. At the end they are sent to "an actual heavy combat situation," which has them rescuing American hostages on foreign soil without ever showing any blood or casualties whatsoever. This comic is more realistic than Marvel's Iraq War superhero comics, but war is still shown as a fun adventure.

As propaganda, these comic books can be said to work very well, especially for readers already in tune with many of the ideas presented—which is one of the main areas where propaganda works, as reinforcement of already accepted ideas.

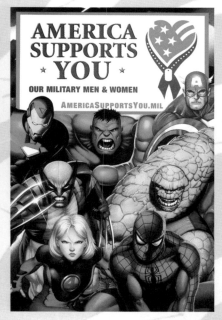

◀ A statement found in all the comics Marvel produced for America Supports You—a division of the American Department of Defense. With heroes like these on your side, you can safely attack any enemy.

◀◀ An evocative image from the end of the story *The Spirit of America*, by Stuart Moore, Cliff Richards, and Joe Pimentel. The American flag is represented four times in this image, with the suit of Captain America as the main focus of the whole page, and the U.S. Army seen steadily advancing.

▶ The cover of one of the comic books that Marvel produced and distributed to the American troops. What more appropriate hero is there to display right at the center of the cover than Captain America—the most famous hero wrapped in the colors of the American flag.

◀ A comic book produced by Marvel Comics in the support of the Army National Guard. This story does not feature any spandex-clad characters, but the average American citizen doing his or her duty in the Army National Guard.

▲ Allison Barber, Deputy Assistant Secretary of Defense for Public Affairs; Defense Secretary Donald H. Rumsfeld; and Marvel Comics Senior Vice President Rob Steffens at the Pentagon for the unveiling of the first of a line of custom-made comic books for members of the American armed services in the Middle East. Photo by Tech. Sgt. Cherie A. Thurlby, USAF.

Saddam Hussein: The Hero

ലോകത്തിലെ എല്ലാ ഇതിഹാസങ്ങളിലും അധ്യാത്മ ക
കഥകളുണ്ട്. അതിന്റെയെല്ലാം അവസാനം നന്മയുടെ പ്ര
ത്രങ്ങളാണ് വിജയം വരിക്കുന്നത്. എന്നാൽ ആധുനിക ക
മാറി. വാണിജ്യവും വ്യവസായികവുമായ സ്വന്തം താൽപ
വാനും വ്യാപിപ്പിക്കുവാനും മഹാശക്തികൾ ആയുധം പ
ഷ്ട്രങ്ങളുടെ ആത്മാഭിമാനത്തെ വ്രണപ്പെടുത്തിക്കൊണ്ട്
നങ്ങൾ പറന്നുയരുന്നു. ഇതാണ് സത്യത്തിൽ നാം ഇറാഖ
ലോകമെങ്ങും ആദരിക്കുന്ന മാർപ്പാപ്പയുടെ സമാധാന ര
ഏറ്റു പറഞ്ഞു. എങ്കിലും അമേരിക്കയുടെ നാമമാത്രമാ
സായികളെ തൃപ്തിപ്പെടുത്തുവാൻ വേണ്ടി അവിടുത്തെ
രികൾ ഇറാക്കിനെതിരെ കൊലവിളി ഉയർത്തി.
പക്ഷെ മാധ്യമങ്ങളൊക്കെയും ഈ കമ്പോള സംസ്കാരര
ക്കയുടെ പോരാട്ടത്തിന് സ്തുതി പാടി. അപ്പോൾ ഇറാ
സദ്ദാം ഹുസൈന്റെ യഥാർത്ഥമുഖം മറച്ചുവെയ്ക്കപ്പെട
മാധ്യമങ്ങളിലൂടെ ഇതുവരെ നിങ്ങൾക്ക് മനസ്സിലാക്കുവ
യഥാർത്ഥ കഥ ചിത്രകഥാ രൂപത്തിൽ ഇവിടെ വായിക്ക

◄◄ Saddam Hussein as the heroic leader, drawn from one of the most widely used images of Saddam. From the collection of Ola Nilsson.

◄ A soldier of the invading/liberating American forces defiles an Iraqi woman by lifting her veil, and is killed for this atrocity by an Iraqi soldier. At the bottom is shown a heroic Saddam Hussein, leading the final defense of Iraq. From the collection of Ola Nilsson.

When looking through Western comics from around the time of the First and Second Gulf Wars (or the Kuwait and Iraq Wars), there is an abundance of portrayals of Saddam Hussein. Considering that he was the leader of the "opposing team," it will probably not surprise anyone that these are not all that flattering. One good example of this is the American comic book *Dictators of the Twentieth Century: Saddam Hussein* by Ted S. Nomura, a two-book series from 2004, where the title says it all. The other dictator of the twentieth century that has been portrayed in this series is Hitler.

But there parts of the world where Saddam Hussein is seen in a somewhat different light. In many countries he is still viewed as a fearless leader who was true to his Arab roots, and in the end was brought down illegally by America. In cartoons from magazines and newspapers in the Arab world, Saddam Hussein is portrayed quite differently than in Western media, although this is not particularly surprising.

A more unexpected vision of Saddam can be found in a biography published as a comic book in India. This story follows Saddam Hussein from his birth, all the way up to his capture by the American soldiers during the Iraq War (or the American invasion, depending on your viewpoint).

The part about Saddam's life up until the attack of the American coalition makes up about half the book, and it is clear that the writer sees Saddam as a hero of his people, born from devout Muslim

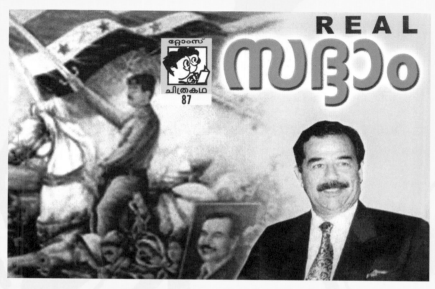

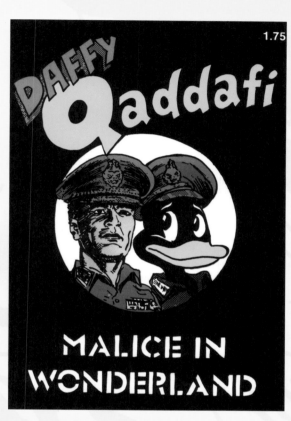

▲ This biography of Saddam Hussein was made by Unnikrishnan Kidagoor, Santhosh Manarcad, and Shaji Marhew, and published as #87 of the Indian comic book *Toms Chithrakatha*. From the collection of Ola Nilsson.

▶ The weird American comic book *Daffy Qaddafi* from 1986 featured another Arab leader who was feared in the West: Muammar Qaddafi. The thin story is a vehicle for the creators to ridicule Qaddafi as much as possible, and the comic ends with Qaddafi hospitalized suffering from a complete mental breakdown with the words: "A little wishful thinking can't hurt—can it?"

parents and a natural leader. The other half tells the story of the war, depicting how vindictive UN inspectors distorted information so that Iraq is falsely accused of harboring "weapons of mass destruction" and finally attacked by overwhelming forces. During all this, Saddam is shown fighting heroically until the bitter end.

There are several strong scenes, like the one where a soldier of the invading force molests a young woman by lifting her veil and is killed by an Iraqi soldier. The most striking scene of all, however, is the final one, in which Saddam is captured after the war. He is shown as calm, almost serene, with his long hair and long beard resembling a holy man, and is also depicted with a light shining out from him. George W. Bush, on

the other hand, is shown as a warmonger, but in a Western suit and not in military gear, backed up by his bombs and a smiling soldier.

The comic was apparently made before the trial and final execution of Saddam, so this is not shown, although it is likely that it was created as a tool of propaganda to sway opinions about Saddam during the trial. The reason for there being such a heroic portrayal of Saddam Hussein in India is that Saddam had a good reputation in that part of the world, and there was a lot of cooperation between India and Iraq during Saddam's reign. He was also known to always make sure that the many guest workers from India, who made up a large part of the work force in Iraq, were treated well.

► Here Andreas makes a case about U.S. military spending. All numbers quoted are referenced and sources are stated in the back of the book, to make sure that the reader takes everything seriously. From the collection of Ola Nilsson.

▲ The book *Addicted to War* is a work in progress. This is an edition of the second, expanded version, published in India. From the collection of Ola Nilsson.

▲ George Bush, Sr. was the head of state when the first edition of *Addicted to War* was published. Here he is seen at the helm of the whole American military force, running down schools and hospitals. Quite a powerful propaganda image. From the collection of Ola Nilsson.

Addicted to War?

▶ **All the powerful men in *Addicted to War* are shown as fat, almost obese males (there are no women) in suits or military uniforms. This to make them recognizable as iconic representatives of the oppressing powers in society, powers that feed off the people. From the collection of Ola Nilsson.**

Most of the examples shown so far in this chapter have been in favor of war, in one way or another (the main exception being *Barefoot Gen*). But there are other views that have been voiced in comics over the years.

One of the largest anti-war manifestations ever in the U.S. was caused by the Vietnam War in the late 1960s and early 1970s, with mass-demonstrations all across the country, as well as in the rest of the world. This coincided with the birth of the underground movement in American comics, a part of the hippie counterculture that was very much against the system in general and consequently also against the war. Some really interesting underground comic books with propaganda messages about the Vietnam War can be found, like *Jesus Meets the Armed Services* by Frank "Foolbert Sturgeon" Stack, in which Jesus is forcibly drafted into the American Army but finally gets tired of being pushed around and simply zaps his tormentors.

Later on, when the underground movement petered out, there were other places where critical voices could be heard. One such place is the magazine *World War 3 Illustrated*, which is edited by Peter Kuper and others, and has been showcasing "dissident" thoughts since its inception in 1980.

Even more recent, and refreshingly unapologetic in its propagandistic intent, is the graphic novel *Addicted to War: Why the U.S. Can't Kick Militarism* by Joel Andreas. This book was first published in 1991, during the Gulf War, and is a merciless attack on the American military policy. Andreas uses the simple and engaging format of the comics to tell quite an intricate story of why the U.S. has such a big army and who profits and who loses from the fact that so much is spent on the military budget.

Following the election of George W. Bush, the invasion of Afghanistan, and the launch of the War on Terror, Andreas saw a need to update his book. It is now sixty-eight pages long and encompasses the world order after September 11. The author tries to show how the expansive history of the U.S. has led to the current situation, where the military budget is larger than the next twenty-five biggest spending countries put together. He also tries to show how corporate business makes a lot of money from this, and that it is the people of the U.S. who suffer the consequences of having to send their sons and daughters into war, at the same time as the government doesn't have enough money for schools and hospitals. Andreas makes a compelling case and backs it up with 145 reference notes to make sure that nobody can accuse him of crying wolf.

The images are often crude but efficient—perhaps because the lack of slick corporate styling signals an honest intent? Men in power are invariably shown as obese and wearing suits, and are contrasted with representatives of the people, most often a young mother and her son. Andreas also mixes the drawn images with photos, to further add to the genuine feel of the story.

Books like these are often produced by enthusiasts and not granted widespread distribution, but according to the cover it has been translated into six languages, with over 70,000 of the Japanese edition and over 200,000 copies of the English edition in print. So the ideas of *Addicted to War* have really reached a big audience.

A panel from *Grenada*, an American comic book about the American-led invasion of Grenada in 1983, carrying a strong anti-Communist message. Here, American troops are portrayed as liberators of the people of Grenada.

Chapter 3

You Dirty, Rotten Commie Bastard!

Communism and the Cold War in Comics

The adventures of

OUR NORMAN

by EVANS

THE BEST OF THE FIRST TWO YEARS

▲ *The Adventures of Our Norman*, a British comic strip by Phil Evans, published in the newspaper *Socialist Worker* in the 1970s. That the aim of this strip was to spread the word of socialism is indicated in the foreword,

where the editor of the *Socialist Worker* writes, "Carry on laughing— that's the one right the bosses and Tories can't take away from us. And, as the man said, he who laughs last, laughs longest."

◄ A Russian poster from 1919, with the title *It Will Not Be Like This Anymore*, published by Publishing House of the Pan-Russia Central Executive Committee of Soviets of Workers', Peasants', Red Army, and Cossacks' Deputies. The text states, "Everything used to be for the capitalist, but the situation has changed. Working people are fighting for their rights."

◄ A page from the American comic book *Watch Out for Big Talk*, published by the National Association of Manufacturers in 1950. Clearly intended to convey the message that any talk of unions or organization of the workers was to be seen as the beginning of a road leading to a Communist and/or fascist society.

Background illustration A page from the comic *Three Men Going Home*, made by the Hong Kong artist Lui Yu-tin in 1955. The story shows three American soldiers going to live in a Communist country out of ideological conviction, but ultimately being shown the ugliness of the Communist system and finally fleeing back.

▶ This book was published in West Berlin in 1974 and contains, as is indicated by the title, a comic depicting and commenting on the first part of Karl Marx's book *Das Kapital*. The worker in the first panels says, "In the last year the prices have gone up 10% and our wages 3%. We demand an adjustment!" The corporate leader answers, "By the Devil, you're a Communist!"

Few things have stirred as much emotion during the twentieth century as Communism. Whether you were pro or con, emotions ran high, and so did the need for propaganda—both to convince your own people of the supremacy of your ideological stance, and to prove to your opponents the folly of their ideas.

These battles of the mind were fought in all kinds of arenas, using every propaganda tool available. The most active period was during the Cold War—so-called because the two major opponents, the U.S. and the Soviet Union, never really engaged directly in war, but were eternally at odds throughout the second half of the twentieth century. Once again, the advent of modern comics coincides with this period, meaning that comics too were used to promote and/or provoke various ideological doctrines. I would divide the comics that have been produced over the years relating to Communism into three general groups.

First and foremost, there is an abundance of American anti-Communist comics, especially from the 1950s—the era of McCarthyism, when anti-Communism saturated every aspect of U.S. society. During this period, practically everyone was seeing Communists in every nook and cranny. Neighbors, friends, and family members were turning each other in. Being summoned to The House Committee on Un-American Activities could destroy your career and subsequently your life. The comics from this era are terribly interesting/scary/hilarious, depending on your viewpoint, and actually worthy of a whole book of their own. I will return to this fascinating era later, in the chapter Social Seduction, but in this chapter I will show a few examples of how this mass hysteria was represented in comics.

Then there is "the other side," Communist countries like the Soviet Union, China, North Korea, Cuba, and so on. Especially after World War II, these countries were very prolific in using propaganda intended for domestic as well as international use. None of these countries (except for China) had a booming comics culture like the one in the U.S., however, and the few comics that were produced with propagandistic intent are scarce and hard to come by. But they are fascinating to read, and I will show a few examples in this chapter, including things that fall mostly under the heading of comic art, where the aesthetics of comics have been used in posters and other media.

Lastly, there are the comics made in the West by people sympathizing with Communist and/or socialist ideas. These are somewhat easier to seek out, and no less interesting to read, as they often have a very open propagandistic approach. This is most likely due to the fact that the creators of these comics are well aware that they are in opposition and the minority, and need to get their message out as clearly as possible.

America Under Communism!

IT WASN'T LONG AFTER THE END OF THE SECOND WORLD WAR, THAT COMMUNIST FORCES IN AMERICA SEIZED THEIR CHANCE. THE STORY IS SAD... THE END TRAGIC... BUT THIS IS THE WAY IT BEGAN...

◄ ◄ The comic book *Is This Tomorrow* was published by the Catechetical Guild in 1950. Notice how the Communist attacks three men: one white, one black, and one priest. This to make sure that as many readers as possible would get the message.

◄ The very suggestive first panel of the comic book *Is This Tomorrow* (notice that there is no question mark after the title). This image is crammed with iconic propaganda messages, like the Soviet flag on top of Capitol Hill, a paramilitary group armed with guns, and two ordinary and unarmed citizens trying to recapture this symbol of the U.S. waving an American flag. Whew!

In the 1950s, the U.S. was a scary place. Many people were convinced that a Communist plot to overthrow the government was imminent and saw conspiracies in every aspect of society. Since these anti-Communist thoughts were accepted by so many, no one was safe from suspicion. Everyone was a suspect and anyone could at any given moment be called in for questioning by The House Committee on Un-American Activities. That alone could cause you to be ostracized by everyone you knew, even if you were not found guilty of anything. In fact, it is compelling how closely U.S. society during the McCarthy era resembled the very Western views of the Communist societies of which they were afraid.

In these rather mad times, some really interesting comics were produced, giving voice to anti-Communist thoughts and trying to convince the reader that the threat was very real indeed, and that vigilance was of the essence. Evocative titles like *Blood Is the Harvest*, *How Stalin Hopes We Will Destroy America*, *If the Devil Would Talk*, and *The*

Red Iceberg tell their own tales. The content was overflowing with propaganda, and just as neurotic as one would expect.

One standout among these comics (and the one with the largest circulation at the time) is the comic book *Is This Tomorrow*, published in 1947 by the Catechetical Guild. This was a publishing house established by Father Louis A. Gales in the 1930s in order to distribute material to further the teachings of the Catholic Church. There is never any doubt as to the message of this comic book, with the headline "To make you THINK!" on the inside cover, followed by revealing text: "Today there are approximately 85,000 official members of the Communist Party in the United States. There are hundreds of additional members whose names are not carried on the Party roles because acting as disciplined fifth columnists of the Kremlin, they have wormed their way into key positions in government offices, trade unions, and other positions of public trust. Communists themselves claim that for every official Party member, there

◄◄ **This scene shows how the Communists finally effect a hostile takeover of Congress, using the military—which has just had its leaders replaced with faithful Communists—to ensure that no one steps out of line. After this, a Communist dictatorship is declared in the U.S.**

◄ **The final blow in** *Is This Tomorrow* **is when a young boy informs on his parents, turning them in for listening to foreign radio broadcasts and worshipping the Madonna in their basement. This is obviously to show how Communism ultimately will destroy even the very fabric (according to the Catholic producers of this comic book) that holds American democracy together: the family.**

are ten others ready, willing, and able to do the Party's bidding. These people are working day and night—laying the groundwork to overthrow YOUR GOVERNMENT!"

And this is exactly what the story is all about. It shows how a small group of dedicated Communists in America take advantage of the unstable situation after a big drought to create unrest, riots, and strikes all across the U.S. Having made sure that the Speaker of the House is on their side, they assassinate both the President and the Vice President and then effectively seize power. After that, they slowly take control of every part of American society, including the military, Congress, and the media. Soon dissidents are being executed right and left, teachers are replaced by people faithful to the Communist Party, the Catholic Church is destroyed, and the workers are forced to do the biddings of the new leaders, or else . . .

This is a scary comic in many ways, particularly since it is easy to see that it would have been quite

convincing at a time when the media was full of reports of Communism, alleged and real, domestic and international. The Communist threat was something everyone was talking about, and the message in a comic like this was quite believable. The fact that parts of the story read like one of the more innovative and improbable "What If" stories from the superhero publisher Marvel Comics was in all likelihood only too easy to ignore.

Is This Tomorrow was one of the first educational/ propagandistic American comics to be as compelling and vivid as its superhero rivals. No matter how horrifying the politics presented might seem today (and it suggests that a good Catholic should not only be anti-Communist, but also anti-union, anti-left, and anti-Hollywood, among other things), it still makes for a compelling read. There were reportedly more than four million copies sold and given away, with Australian and French-Canadian editions as well, making it one of the more powerful and far-reaching examples of anti-Communist propaganda.

Background illustration **These panels show how the American Communists pit different groups against each other in order to create pandemonium and lay the grounds for a hostile takeover. The Communists use the unions to paralyze U.S. industry. They also create riots, pitting white against black, Gentile against Jew, and so on.**

This Godless Communism

The Red Scare continued for quite some time in the U.S., although the real mania of the McCarthy era waned as the 1950s gave way to a new decade. The notion of a Communist conspiracy on the move to take over the U.S. was still kept alive, in, among other things, the children's comic book *Treasure Chest of Fun and Fact*.

Treasure Chest was a biweekly comic book with (mostly overtly) Catholic-oriented content, published by George A. Pflaum and distributed to parochial schools from 1946 to 1972. The comics were often religious, but not exclusively so. They could deal with historical moments, the feats of sports heroes, the lives of saints, physics, and sometimes even politics—as in the infamous series of stories *This Godless Communism*. This series was published during 1961, almost fifteen years after *Is This Tomorrow*, and even though a lot had changed, much had not. The series begins with a chapter showing how life would be in a Communist America, which is quite similar to the ideas shown in *Is This Tomorrow*.

After this, the series gives a historical background to Communism, with brief biographies of Marx, Lenin, and Stalin, ending with the story of how Nikita Khrushchev—the Soviet leader at the time the tale was produced—struggled for and gained power. These chapters are presented as recounting historical facts, which they mostly do, but these facts are of course chosen to make the reader draw negative conclusions from them, and are almost always complemented with snide or critical remarks to show the folly of it all—quite effective as a means of propaganda.

This ten-chapter feature was drawn by the artist Reed Crandall, best remembered for drawing the character Blackhawk for DC Comics and other comics for the publisher EC. He was for many years one of the main artists working on *Treasure Chest*, and his craftsmanship in both drawing and visual storytelling is part of what makes *This Godless Communism* such a compelling read still.

This comic is really a gem when read today, because it contains so many clues to the way the world was perceived in the U.S. in the early 1960s. You get a clear feeling of how the author must have felt when stating that forty percent of the world was under the influence of the Communists, especially the sheer urgency with which he perceived that he needed to press these anti-Communist ideas on new generations of school children.

But perhaps the crowning glory of *This Godless Communism* is on the inside cover of the very first issue. There can be found a letter stating, among other things, that "Communism represents the most serious threat facing our way of life." The letter is signed by John Edgar Hoover, Director of the FBI.

◄ A panel from the very last episode of *This Godless Communism*, where the creators try to recap the whole series. Here we see the leader of the Soviet Union in 1961, Nikita Khrushchev, showing the "two faces of Communism": threatening war to those he needs to intimidate, and promising peace to those he believes will listen to that.

▶ The beautiful cover of the first issue of *Treasure Chest of Fun and Fact* with the series *This Godless Communism*. Notice that this magazine sported the seal of approval of the Comics Code Authority. This type of religion-based comic book, whose aim was to educate the readers, was the very epitome of what this self-censor bureau was all about.

▼ The very first story of *This Godless Communism* shows how life would have been for a normal American family in a Communist United States. Here we see how the teachings in the schools change to suit the new world order. Note the flag for the "U.S.S.A."

▶ A description of the dreaded Comintern (Communist International), a group whose aim it was to spread Communism all over the world. These panels might seem almost paranoid by today's standard, but the Comintern is a historical fact, and even though it had been officially dissolved by the time this comic was published, most historians agree that the network it established was still in existence.

▲ Here the creators of *This Godless Communism* let Nikita Khrushchev say exactly what many Americans of this period feared, that the idea of Communism would be spread and accepted by the people of the world. The last picture of Khrushchev is not very flattering, to say the least.

Imperialist Ideology in the Disney Comics?

DORFMAN & MATTELART

HOW TO READ DONALD DUCK

$3.25
£1.35

NATIONAL BANK
DEPOSITOS NOCTURNOS

IMPERIALIST IDEOLOGY
IN THE DISNEY
COMIC

◄ *How to Read Donald Duck: Imperialist Ideology in the Disney Comics*, by Dorfman and Mattelart. A worn and tattered copy of the English language edition, from 1975.

▲ Disney comics are also published in Arab countries. Here, a beautiful, specially designed cover with Donald sporting a fez, a potent symbol of Muslim identity. The stories in these comic books are the same as in their Western counterparts, however.

▶ **The first sequence of the story *Want to Buy an Island?* by Carl Barks from 1960. These panels are shown in *How to Read Donald Duck* as examples of how capitalism and imperialism are constantly put forth as the ideal values upon which our world should be built. From the collection of Germund von Wowern.**

Background illustration **A telltale scene from the story *The Great Wig Mystery* by Carl Barks from 1964, used by Mattelart and Dorfman to show how imperialist ideas are sold to the reader through the Disney comics. In this story, Africans are shown as easily beguiled, primitive savages, ready to sell their positions for the trinkets the ducks have brought, speaking in a "funny," derogatory accent, and living in a country (Kooko Coco) whose capital city consists of "three straw huts and some moving haystacks." From the collection of Germund von Wowern.**

I have included a great many comics in this book that might not seem to be propaganda to some readers (although which ones will probably vary). In fact, what is and what isn't propaganda is quite often very subjective and depends on the ideological, religious, and other beliefs of the viewer. Disney comics, for instance, would be perceived by most readers as harmless children's fare. This is not necessarily so, however, if you live in a Communist or even socialist country.

Disney comics today are created and mostly consumed in Europe, with Denmark and Italy as the main centers of production. But this has not always been the case, and between the 1930s and 1970s Disney comics were produced in the U.S. and spread from there all over the world. When anti-American feelings flared up, especially during the Vietnam War, these comics were seen in parts of the world as spreading American ideas and ideology. The main proponents of these theories were two academics working in Chile, Ariel Dorfman and Armand Mattelart, who in the early 1970s wrote the widely influential book *Para Leer al Pato Donald*, which was published in various languages across the world. In English it was named *How to Read Donald Duck: Imperialist Ideology in the Disney Comic*, published in 1975. *How to Read Donald Duck* is interesting for several reasons. It was one of the first serious, academic studies of comics, and certainly one of the first made from a pronounced political viewpoint.

Dorfman and Mattelart used Marxist theory to look at the Disney comics published in South America, and arrived at the conclusion that they conveyed an imperialist ideology to the readers. Some of the authors' theories seem a bit dated today, and sometimes they take their theories a bit too far, but on the whole they present a compelling case.

The most damaging examples are found in the comics where Uncle Scrooge, Donald, and the nephews travel to other parts of the world. Here it is evident that the "natives" they meet are shown as little more than children, clearly positioned below these visitors from a more advanced culture and open to exploitation in the name of capitalism. The chain of evidence becomes more muddled when Dorfman and Mattelart try to show that the reason there are almost no parents in the Disney world (they are all nephews, uncles, and so on)

is not only due to Disney wanting to exclude sex from their world, but also that removing the family ties creates horizontal levels in the society, with no hierarchic order except the ones given by the amount of money someone possesses. This, the authors state, leads to a situation where there is no solidarity and the only thing left is harsh competition. Here, I must confess, they start to lose me.

Dorfman and Mattelart's main argument is that these Disney comics are not only a reflection of the prevailing capitalist ideology in the U.S., but that their creators were actually aware of this and worked as active agents in spreading this ideology. Considering that most of the examples shown are by Carl Barks, and reading interviews with him, this is perhaps taking it too far, even though he seems to have been quite a reactionary man who believed in the American way.

A number of critiques have been raised against the theories put forward by Dorfman and Mattelart, especially since the texts in the comics they are discussing are sometimes distorted due to overzealous translators for the publication in South America. This mars some of the authors' discussions, but it doesn't obscure the fact that these comics do portray the world according to a fundamentally capitalist viewpoint, or that they were seen as quite provocative propaganda by readers in South America.

All images shown here from Disney comics are the same as shown in Dorfman and Mattelart's book, here with the original texts.

Chinese Propaganda Comics

China has one of the longest continuous artistic traditions in the world, and telling stories with pictures is part of that great tradition. There were many precursors, but the development of modern Chinese cartoons began in the early 1800s and was augmented by the introduction of Western printing methods in the latter part of the century—boosting the circulations of prints and making it possible to reach a wider audience.

The main format for comics in China has for a long time been the so-called lianhuanua, or "linked pictures"—picture stories printed in small, pocket-sized books with text below or above the images. The covers were printed in color, and the insides in black and white, with one large image per page. The stories—often originally inspired by traditional Chinese tales and later on also by popular books and films—were condensed and presented in a format suited for an audience with a lesser degree of reading ability.

When the Communists took over in 1949, they increased the production of these comics as an ideological and cultural weapon. Some modern, American comics had been imported before that, so the ideas of using balloons to convey speech and thought, using onomatopoetic words to convey sound, etc., were present, but the artists making lianhuanua mostly preferred the older method of printing texts and images separately.

The lianhuanua comic books have been widely spread throughout most parts of China. In the 1970s, it is reported that many volumes had print runs in the hundreds of thousands, sometimes reaching over a million with several print runs of a single volume. They were produced and distributed provincially by the People's Art Institute in the different regional capitals. In the 1970s the People's Art Institute of Shanghai alone printed sixteen million copies a year—in Beijing the number was thirty million—and they were sold just about everywhere, handed out as recreation during train rides and so on. One reason for the proliferation of comics in China was perhaps that the written

◄ The cover of a traditional Chinese comic book, a so-called lianhuanua, small pamphlets that consist of a color cover and black and white interiors with one image per page.

language was the same, and that no matter what dialect someone spoke almost everyone could read these comics.

Generally there has not been a lot of difference between lianhuanua comics made for children and for adults. They simply tell stories, and these are mostly realistic, either about historical events or everyday life in the present day. After the Communists came to power, the so-called "Red comics" were made with the express purpose of educating the readers and teaching them the correct, revolutionary way of looking at things. If a comic deviated ever so slightly from the right, Maoist way, it was destroyed. In the 1960s, for instance, there were hundreds of lianhuanua comic books produced by the "black" anti-Mao movement, but they were quickly taken out of circulation.

When looking for propaganda in comics, going through lianhuanua is like hitting the mother lode. Here you can find every kind of propaganda, from the very subtle to the overtly obvious. The stories express Communist views of the world, showing the struggles of the poor under capitalism and very often striking displays of working-class heroism. There has even been a lianhuanua comic book about the life and times of Lenin.

Background illustration A picture from the lianhuanua comic book *Bravery on the Deep Blue Seas*, made in 1965 with a print run of 200,000. The story was based on a book by Liang Xin, adapted by Wan Jia-chun, and drawn by Xu Jin. This example is taken from an English translation from the 1970s. From the collection of Caj Byqvist.

▼ Two issues of a Chinese comic book from 1974 with beautiful propaganda covers. The comics within are full of stories of heroic workers, often women, showing how China was built.

► One of the paintings that comprises the picture story *The Long March*, made by the artist Zhang Sheng in 1976. It was made to commemorate the historical Long March in 1936, when Mao Zedong initiated the movement that would eventually lead to the creation of the People's Republic of China in 1949.

连环画报

一九七四年三月号
总第六期

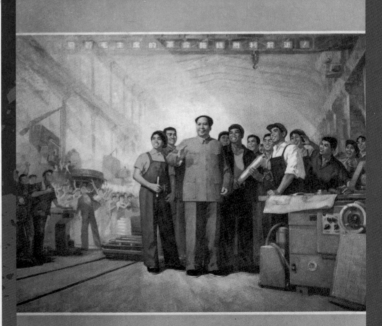

连环画报

一九七四年
十月号

▼ The comic book *Design for Survival* was published in several versions. Here is one that was aimed at a general audience—sporting a traditional comic book cover—and a version that was included with a newspaper, thus given a more somber, fact-filled look.

► A beautiful piece of propaganda, using every trick possible. On this page there are several scary visions of Communist dominance, unconcealed displays of ideological positions, and even a reference to Hitler, the ultimate bad guy.

◄ When making propaganda, it is often practical to use well-known images and icons that people already have an understanding of. Here the historical allegory of the Trojan horse is used to show what the results will be of signing agreements of disarmament with the Communists, who will eventually reveal that they did not disarm at all.

► The first image in the comic book version of *Design for Survival*, which sets the tone for the whole story. The Cuban Missile Crisis is referred to again and again as the perfect example of how "dynamic deterrence" works, scaring the enemy, i.e. the Communists, into backing away.

Design for Survival

During the Cold War, the arms race between the U.S. and the U.S.S.R. was a seemingly never-ending battle. In the end, most historians agree that it was the aggressive build-up of the American military forces by President Ronald Reagan during the 1980s that finally broke the Soviets and laid the groundwork for the Perestroika, and ultimately the fall of Communist rule in the Soviet Union.

This is, however, a hotly debated subject, as can be seen for instance in Chapter 2: Addicted to War. During the Cold War, there were attempts to break this arms race with various disarmament programs. These were often viewed as dangerous, even unpatriotic, by the government, and especially by the military. One of the most potent of all propaganda efforts in favor of the American build-up of a nuclear force greater than that of the Soviet Union was a book written by four-star General Thomas S. Power called *Design for Survival*.

Power was not just any general, but a decorated war hero, a former Commander in Chief of the Strategic Air Command, and Director of the Joint Strategic Target Planning Staff. He was for more than seven years the man with the "finger on the trigger" of U.S. nuclear defense. To say the least, he was a person whose ideas were listened to, and the book spent some time on the bestseller lists when it was released in 1965. Eventually, it also got turned into a comic book.

The comic book *Design for Survival* was drawn by cartoonist Bill Lignante, and it often quotes more or less directly from the original book. It is all very well made, and quite a convincing read. It is also very, very indicative of the times in which it was produced. This is another example where there were absolutely no holds barred when it came to using various tools from the propaganda toolbox. *Design for Survival* is one thirty-two-page long speech by Power (he is always either seen behind a speaker's podium, or being interviewed on TV), showing everything from nightmarish visions of Communist rule in America to strange new Soviet weapons, including a device that seems to be focusing solar rays to a specific spot in the U.S., and a strange round device with atomic warheads sticking out at all angles, which looks like something out of a James Bond movie.

Throughout the comic book, Power makes his case for the build-up of "a balanced complex of diversified weapons systems" to act as "deterrence through superior military strength." This message is sold with some really heavy anti-Communist rhetoric. In the end, the message seems to be that the American people should just make sure that the Strategic Air Command gets more funding and leave the world order to them, which is a pretty hard sell. But General Power does a good job of it. Despite the fact that much of the content today feels like heavy propaganda and not a little paranoid, this comic book, and the original, were probably quite effective at the time in persuading the American people of the necessity of building the American armed forces and its nuclear bombs.

THE LESSON OF CUBA

IN THE CUBAN CRISIS, OUR STRATEGIC AIR COMMAND BOMBERS ON AIRBORNE ALERT FLEW OVER 20 MILLION MILES, ARMED AND READY TO STRIKE ON COMMAND FROM THE PRESIDENT.... AN UMBRELLA OF OVERWHELMING STRENGTH, UNDER WHICH THE UNITED STATES DEMANDED THAT KHRUSHCHEV WITHDRAW THE RUSSIAN MISSILES!

MOSCOW

CUBA

Collecting the Cuban Conundrum

In many Communist countries, comics have never (despite the attractive alliteration) been a preferred media through which to spread information or propaganda. This is surprising, seeing that comics, as is shown throughout this book, with their instant appeal and the ease with which they can be read by almost everyone, are perfect tools for transmitting ideas and convincing readers of various ideologies. Perhaps it has something to do with the medium being too readily associated with the "enemy"— i.e. America.

In Cuba, for instance, the major children's magazine, *Zunzún*, mostly contains illustrated text, with only a few examples of comics. These texts are certainly fascinating, featuring, among other things, biographies of famous Communist leaders from around the world, but they are not comic art in any way, shape, or form. Something closer to comics can be found in a series of illustrated collectors' cards, which are meant to be pasted into albums to form a kind of comic book called *Album de la Revolución Cubana 1952–1959*.

The format of this item is interesting in itself. It is an album, with squares marking where color pictures are supposed to be glued in. Beneath every square there is a caption of one or two sentences. Together they form a comic with chapters that are between one and six pages long. This format, with images and text printed separately, is something that was abandoned a long time ago in Western comics, when speech bubbles, onomatopoetic words, and symbols for motion and sound all revolutionized the comics form. Add to that the fact that the reproduction looks like everything has been copied, recopied, and recopied again many times, and the overall feeling is that of something from another world.

Revolución Cubana contains exactly what you would expect considering the title. It is an account of what happened between the very first, unsuccessful attack on the Moncada military base on July 26, 1953 (thus giving the name for the revolutionary

organization the 26th of July Movement, led by Fidel Castro) all the way through to the triumphant entering into Havana in January 1959. The series of pictures was originally published in 1960–1961, just shortly after the events took place, and given away with the purchase of various food products. The way these events are shown is of course very propagandistic, with emphasis on the heroic acts of the revolutionaries, the immoral deeds of the dictator Batista, and the support and sympathy of the people.

Still, looking through this book and comparing it with similar items from China or Russia, there is not a total focus on the heroic acts of the great leader, Fidel Castro. Maybe it was too early for that in 1960–1961. It is, on the contrary, made clear that the victory was won by several leaders, including Raúl Castro, Camilo Cienfuegos, and Ernesto "Che" Guevara. The middle spread of the book contains "idol portraits" of all the revolutionary

▲ The book *Album de la Revolución Cubana 1952–1959* was originally produced in the early 1960s, and tells the story of the revolution as seen through the eyes of the victors of the conflict, naturally. The image hovering over Fidel Castro is the face of José Martí, a Cuban hero, poet, and revolutionary from the nineteenth century.

▼ One page from *Revolución Cubana*, depicting parts of the battle of Sierra Maestra, and also showing that there were quite a lot of prominent women fighting for the revolution, most notably Celia Sánchez. Note the revolutionary symbols between the glued-in pictures.

▼ The cover of *Zunzún*, the major children's magazine in Cuba. This is a special edition, devoted solely to the life of the young "Ernestito," who would later become Che Guevara to the world.

Here we see the separate groups of Cuban revolutionaries entering Havana after the hostilities were ended. Picture 258 shows Camilo Gienfuego's troops, 259 depicts Che Guevara and his famous 8th division, and finally 260 shows Fidel Castro's triumphant arrival after a long victory march across Cuba.

leaders, photos showing an array of surprisingly young bearded men. Of all the sixteen depicted, only Fidel, his brother Raúl, and a few others survived to become old bearded men. Most were either accused of being anti-revolutionary and summarily shot or had inexplicable accidents and died in mysterious circumstances. It's a hard life being a revolutionary . . .

The strangest thing about *Revolución Cubana* for a Western reader is the multitude of realistic violence shown in the images. People are tortured, executed, and killed all over the place. Obviously on one level this is not so strange, since the revolution in Cuba was a bloody one, but it is not something usually associated with collectors' cards and comics. OK, so the average superhero comic is just as violent—it's just that *this* violence actually feels real.

Octobriana

One of the strangest stories ever told about a comic's origin is the one about the well-endowed Soviet superheroine Octobriana, created by a group of dissident artists in the U.S.S.R. They called themselves PPP, standing for Progressive Political Pornography. The group consisted of young people who were disillusioned with the way Communism had evolved and wanted to express themselves in ways that were not permitted. During the 1960s they started an underground magazine called *Mtsyry*, which was professionally printed. These early Soviet fanzines were called samizdat (sam: self; izdat: to publish) and consisted of material produced, duplicated, and distributed illegally.

For *Mtsyry*, the group, among other things, created the character Octobriana, named after the October Revolution of 1917. The name was loosely seen as meaning "the Spirit of the October Revolution," and was based on the notion of the young idealists in the PPP; that the principles of the Communist revolution were absolutely right, but that Lenin's ideals had been perverted by Stalin and other power-hungry and bloodthirsty "heirs" to authority in the U.S.S.R. Octobriana was created to embody the true principles of the October Revolution, acting not on behalf of the Soviet Union but of mankind. Visually Octobriana was based on a major sex symbol of the time, Brigitte Bardot, augmented with Mongolian features and given a big red star on her forehead.

We might never have known of Octobriana had it not been for the Czech Petr Sadecky, who on several occasions traveled to Russia, took part in the activities of the PPP, and managed to smuggle some of their artwork into the West. Using that art, and telling his own story, he produced the book

▲ The cover of the book that showed the world the art of the dissident Russian group PPP, Progressive Political Pornography. Or did it? Published in 1971, it caused a big stir and led a lot of artists, like the American Trina

Robbins and British Bryan Talbot, to create comics featuring Octobriana. From the collection of Nils Kroon.

▶ Octobriana, in her full glory. She was described as a Russian version of Barbarella—the sultry SF-heroine of both comics and film (played by Jane Fonda) in the 1960s, a description which seems to fit rather well. From the collection of Nils Kroon.

Octobriana and the Russian Underground, which was published in 1971. It caused a minor storm when released.

Since the character Octobriana was the product of dissident artists working within the Soviet Union, she was not copyrighted; she was even meant to be freely used by anyone. This led to Octobriana appearing in a variety of other incarnations, such as in the science fiction graphic novel *The Adventures of Luther Arkwright* by the British cartoonist Bryan Talbot, and as a tattoo on the rock singer Billy Idol's arm.

Now if all this sounds almost too good to be true, that's because it probably is. It has been suggested that Petr Sadecky created the character Octobriana himself, spreading the story about PPP as a way of promoting his own comics. He is said to have enlisted the help of two Czech artists, Bohumil Konečný and Zdenek Burian, to create a comic about the character "Amazona." Sadecky then managed to escape to the West, bringing the artwork with him, and in an effort to sell his comics he changed the name to Octobriana, added a red star on her forehead, and turned it all into a fake political statement.

There is evidence of this; for instance, the fact that the character is still called Amazona in one of the printed pages and that Burian and Konečný sued Sadecky in a West German court, winning the case but never recovering all of their stolen artwork.

Whatever the truth might be—and we are not likely to know since Petr Sadecky seems to have vanished after the publication of *Octobriana and the Russian Underground* and is supposed to have died in Germany in 1991—this character still fascinates. In the UK, several comic books have been published during the last decade featuring her. So, fake or not, this Communist semi-goddess is still a potent symbol.

▶▼ The first two panels of a comic that the PPP supposedly produced in 1962, predicting the Soviet invasion of Czechoslovakia six years before it actually happened. However, since the book *Octobriana and the Russian Underground* was published in 1971, three years after the invasion, this claim cannot be substantiated. From the collection of Nils Kroon.

Background illustration Octobriana with PPP favorite, Lenin. In this story, Octobriana follows Lenin on his last walk across the snowy park alongside the Kremlin.

As the temperature drops, Lenin freezes into the gesture of the famous statue, recognized around the world. From the collection of Nils Kroon.

▶ The imaginative flying vehicle of Octobriana, here seen emptying its refuse chute with the empty bottles of the heroine and her crew's favorite drink. A bigger clash of symbols could probably not be assembled in one single comics panel, at least not during the Cold War. From the collection of Nils Kroon.

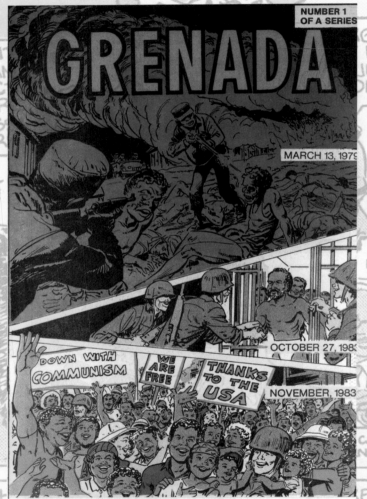

▲ There were no holds barred when this cover was produced. At the top, a vivid image of the coup that turned Grenada into a Communist dictatorship; in the middle, American soldiers rescuing political prisoners; and at the bottom, the people of Grenada celebrating with their saviors.

▲▲ A beautiful summing up of the CIA's view. The slogan "Backward Ever, Forward Never" is a distortion of a quote by one of the Communist leaders of Grenada, Maurice Bishops: "Forward Ever, Backward Never."

▲ How the fledgling Communists of Grenada were educated in the Soviet Union and prepared for the takeover of the country.

Grenada

This comic book is one of the standout examples of propaganda in comics, for several reasons. It is a short, sixteen-page story about the American-led invasion/liberation of the small Caribbean island of Grenada in 1983. The invasion was prompted by a Communist coup, and that this was very much part of the Cold War is indicated by the fact that the American troops, who outnumbered their opponents by four to one, were met not only by Grenadian forces but also by Cuban soldiers and Soviet "advisors."

The comic book *Grenada*, with the subtitle *Rescued from Rape and Slavery*, is so heavily loaded with propaganda that it is almost comical. It features a normal Grenadian family feeling the repercussions of the Communist takeover, and uttering things like, "They're Communist rats! The People's Revolutionary Government is nothing but a puppet of Castro's Cuba! Russia orders and Castro pulls the puppet strings!" After the invasion and the rescue, we get the story of a political prisoner, Antonio Langdon, who tells us of all the horrible things the Communists did, going through everything in excruciating detail, and ending it all with a plea to all the other small countries in the Caribbean to be on the alert against Communism. No doubt much of what is shown is actually true, but the anti-Communist sentiment that saturates every image and every word makes the whole comic . . . well, cheesy. It's hard to see how the producers of *Grenada* actually could believe that anyone would be convinced by such overstated and obvious propaganda.

Grenada is often presented as the comic book that the CIA dropped from airplanes over the island prior to or just after the invasion. This information is all over the internet, but when actually reading the comic, that claim doesn't seem very likely. For one thing, the copyright is 1984, the year after the invasion. Another damning fact is that the comic, and even the cover, depicts what actually happened, with correct dates and other information. Considering that the American-led

◄ **The relieved citizens of Grenada welcoming their rescuers. In a later scene, one of them actually utters the incredible line: "Hooray! We are free! God bless daddy Reagan! God bless America!"**

invasion took place just five days after the Communist coup, it is not very likely that this whole comic book was written, drawn, and printed in this time. More likely, it was produced afterwards, to convince Americans, Grenadians, or other readers that the invasion was the right thing to do.

Another interesting story about this unsigned comic book is that it was produced by Malcolm Ater and his company Commercial Comics Inc., and that when he was supposed to get paid by his employer, he was told to go to Washington D.C., where he met with a CIA agent in a taxi and was given $35,000 in cash in a suitcase. Whether the last part is true, I cannot say, but it does seem likely that Ater, a professional maker of educational and political comics, produced the book, and that it was commissioned by the CIA.

This is, of course, never stated in the comic itself, and on the inside cover a message from A. C. Langdon (the political prisoner cited in the book) declares that: "The V.O.I.C.E. (Victims of International Communist Emissaries) is sponsoring this booklet to warn you of the imminent totalitarian danger to your right as human beings. This danger is posed by the cunning advocates of change . . . violent change that subscribes to the theme of Forward Never, Backward Ever." It is ended with an exhortation to the reader to "THINK! THINK AND STAY FREE!" Well, any reader doing exactly that will not readily accept the other messages in this propaganda comic.

Background illustration **A lesson in regional politics, again from an American, anti-Communist perspective. The former political prisoner Antonio Langdon is here made to warn the other Caribbean countries of the threat of Communism.**

Brought to Light?

The 1980s was a decade full of political scandals, accusations, and "affairs" involving the U.S. government. The Iran-Contra affair was perhaps the most damaging one, where it was proven that representatives for the U.S. brokered a deal to sell weapons to Iran in exchange for the release of American hostages, and then used the money made in that illegal deal to support the Contras in Nicaragua.

A precursor to the actual "affair"—made famous by the hearings with, among others, Oliver North—was a lawsuit filed by the Christic Institute against the U.S. government. The Christic Institute was a public-interest law firm, specializing in representing "the little guy" against big corporations and other imposing groups. In this case, which became their most widely publicized, they represented two journalists: Martha Honey and Tony Avirgan. They had investigated the so-called La Penca bombing, which happened during the Nicaraguan civil war in 1984, and which saw several Western journalists killed and the leader of the Contras, Edén Pastora, wounded. Honey and Avirgan claimed their investigation showed that reputed CIA contract employee John Floyd Hull had been among those involved. The charges were finally thrown out of court by the judge, and the costs of the proceedings bankrupted the Christic Institute, but many of the names in the lawsuit later turned up in the Iran-Contra affair.

A lot of people were actively following this lawsuit, and one example of the public interest is the book *Brought to Light: A Graphic Docudrama*, which was published in 1988. This book contains two comics, made separately by different artistic teams but both based on material from the lawsuit. One of the comics, *Flashpoint: The La Penca Bombing* by Joyce Brabner and Thomas Yeates, tries to present the facts from the lawsuit as correctly and objectively as possible. The other, *Shadowplay: The Secret Team* by Alan Moore and Bill Sienkiewicz, is a more allegorical and openly subjective political statement about the involvement of the CIA in just about everything since World War II.

Of the two comics, there is no question as to which one leaves a more lasting impression. In *Shadowplay*, Alan Moore excels in telling his story in a way that is hard to read without being moved. For instance, early on he establishes that an Olympic swimming pool can hold 20,000 gallons, and compares this to the fact that an adult human body holds about one gallon of blood. This is then used repeatedly as a visual measure of how many victims various CIA activities have yielded. Very effective, as this image stays in your mind long after you've finished reading. That the story is narrated by an anthropomorphic American eagle, depraved, drunken, and even high on drugs but still proud of its achievements around the world, only enhances its effectiveness.

So, does this book constitute propaganda? Yes, definitely, since it so clearly tries to convince the reader of the truths presented within its covers. The fact that it is stated, at the end of the introduction, that the lawsuit was on appeal at the time of the printing also implies the intent was to convince the readers not only of the wrongdoings of the CIA, but of the righteousness of the lawsuit in question.

▼ The book *Brought to Light: A Graphic Docudrama* was published as a so-called flip-cover, with two books in one, each readable from one end of the book.

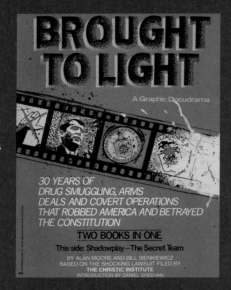

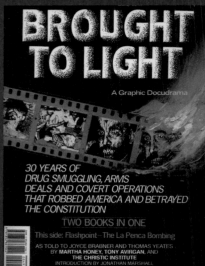

▼ The map presented in the middle of the book, where the two comics meet. On it are marked various unlawful activities conducted by the CIA, all according to the declaration of the Christic Institute.

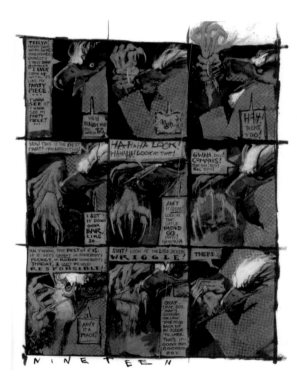

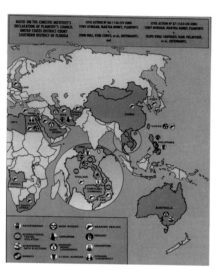

▲ In *Shadowplay: The Secret Team*, Alan Moore and Bill Sienkiewicz show the U.S. as a degenerate American eagle (as seen in the symbol for the CIA) in a bar, bragging about his accomplishments through the CIA. Here we see a scene were the eagle rips off his own hand and shows how it can move on its own, without the eagle being blamed. This is used as an allegory for the allegation that the CIA, in a private capacity, rehired many of the shady operatives that the Carter administration had fired.

▶ The story in *Flashpoint: The La Penca Bombing* is a straightforward retelling of the circumstances surrounding the infamous bombing and the investigation carried out by the reporters Martha Honey and Tony Avirgan. Here we see reproductions of the comics that the CIA produced and distributed for the Contras.

The Adventures of Tintin: The Anarchist!

▲ *The Adventures of Tintin: Breaking Free* has been published several times and this latest printing is still readily available through all the major internet bookshops.

▲ Tintin throws himself into the melee of a strike turned into a riot, and gives "the old Bill" a wallop.

◄ "The Captain" speaking out about the need for a class war. That the creator of *Breaking Free* chose to use the characters from *The Adventures of Tintin* was obviously to get attention, but also to provoke the readers when these well-known characters do and say things we wouldn´t expect them to.

When Hergé first drew Tintin in the late 1920s, he could not possibly have been aware that his creation would become one of the most easily recognizable characters ever produced for comics. Be that as it may, today Tintin is an icon, and even though Hergé stipulated in his will that no one was allowed to draw him after his creator had gone to meet his maker, an ever growing number of new comics featuring Tintin have been produced over the years. Most of them are fan-based, published in secret—since the heirs to Hergé guard their property vigorously—and the stories are puerile fantasies where Tintin engages in all kinds of carnal pleasure that he didn't even think about in the original comics. And then there is *The Adventures of Tintin: Breaking Free*.

Breaking Free is a graphic novel in which the unnamed creator (using the pseudonym J. Daniels—perhaps trying to invoke the feeling of a famous whiskey) actually tells a coherent, interesting story and uses the iconic powers of Tintin for a purpose beyond that of imitating and satirizing. The publisher of this book was the anarchist organization Attack International, and it is dedicated to "all those fighting against capitalism," which says quite a lot about the content.

It is the story of a young British man—bearing a remarkable resemblance to Tintin—who has been fired for punching his boss and gets a job at a construction site with the help of his uncle, "the Captain"—modeled after Captain Haddock. They both witness how their co-worker Joe Hill (probably named after the famous Anarcho-syndicalist organizer with the same name) falls to the ground and dies due to negligent safety measures on the site. In a furor over the insensitive response to this by their manager, the workers instigate a strike for better working conditions. The owners of the company and the corrupt representatives of the workers' union try to stop them, but the strike slowly grows as other groups of workers follow. Soon the whole nation is in uproar, with the British government in a panic using more and more militant means to try and stop the uprising. Finally we see Tintin and the Captain leading a demonstration with hundreds of thousands of people and talking about taking over the whole country.

This may sound like a glorified and romantic vision of public uprising and the downfall of capitalism, but it is actually quite a well-told story, given its didactic purposes. When it was first published in Great Britain in 1988, it created quite a stir and had many of the major newspapers crying out about the inappropriate way in which the book uses the innocent face of Tintin to sell anarchistic and subversive ideas (some of them are cited on the back of later printings of the book). But neither this criticism, nor the restraining attempts by the heirs of Hergé, has stopped *Breaking Free* from being reprinted at least twice. Anyone who wants to publish it, by the way, can do so for free since it is stated on the inside cover that, "This book or any part of it may be freely reproduced by any revolutionary group. But copyright protects it from being poached by capitalists, etc."

► **The final image shows Tintin, the Captain, and his wife Mary in a silhouette with raised fists and Tintin holding an assault weapon. Quite a long way from the certainly idealistic but still mostly harmless character that Hergé created.**

Chapter 4
Social Seduction

Social Engineering Through Comics

Most of the comics that I have chosen to display in this book so far carry a lot of negative connotations—at least for most people. I have shown comics used to promote racism, war, Communism, anti-Communism, and so on. But as I outlined in the introduction, using my rather broad definition of propaganda there is no need for the comic's message to be something deemed bad, evil, or dangerous in order for it to be included here. On the contrary, propaganda in comics can, in my book, be whatever anyone tries to convince anyone else of—whether "good" or "bad"— through comics.

To prove my point, in this chapter I have collected together some really interesting comics that might to the average reader seem to be mostly informational and/or educational—not at first glance overtly propagandistic. Well, as I have stated before, it's all in the eye of the beholder . . .

Many institutions, organizations, and government bureaucracies have seen fit to use comics over the years to tell us how we should live our lives. The aim is to influence popular attitudes and social behavior, and thus it can be considered a form of social engineering. Many of these comics are on the theme of "Thou shalt not . . ." We have, for instance, been told not to smoke, not to drink, not to use drugs, not to have sex outside of marriage, and so on. Often these messages have been hammered in rather bluntly with comics made by people caring perhaps a bit too much about the message and too little about the presentation.

are examples in this chapter, with various people arguing for and against drugs, atomic energy, the killing of animals, and so on. Pitting these comics against each other, often on the same spread, makes you realize that many of them were not made to convince the other side, but rather to enforce the feelings of the "home team." That is an important function of propaganda, too; sometimes the most important.

No matter if you agree with the things the cartoonists creating these comics want to tell you (or rather, as is more often the case, with the

◄ An informational American comic from 1956, using the art of Al Capp, including his incredibly popular character Li'l Abner on the cover. The comics inside told the reader how to act if a natural disaster hits their part of the world. The art inside the book was not, probably to the dismay of many readers, made by Capp.

Background illustration In the fifteen issues of *King Features Career Educational Series* from the early 1970s, the character Popeye told the young readers about various careers that they could aspire to, such as construction, marketing and distribution, and transportation. My favorite is the one about "Communication and Media Careers," considering this character's aptitude

► In Sweden, all children read the comic *Bamse*. Here, the Swedish fire authority has used the iconic status of the character Bamse and commissioned a special comic book for children about safety measures in case of a fire. The title translates as "Bamse's Fire School."

◄ The front cover of the underground comic book *Net Profit*, published in 1974 as the first of a proposed series of "Ecomix." The most hard-hitting story in this comic book is *How I Became a Horrible Porpoise-Killing Monster*, which tells the (supposedly true) story of a young man signing up on a tuna trawler and experiencing the real horrors of the way dolphins were treated.

▲ This comic book was part of a series focusing on energy, and was published in association with the Walt Disney Company, using the famous characters Mickey Mouse and Goofy to talk about energy preservation. On the cover of this particular issue, it is evident who was paying for these comics, and the uncritical way in which oil production and consumption was dealt with makes this even more clear.

Crime Does Not Pay!

▶ This cover of a 1947 issue of *Crime Does Not Pay* boasts a large number of reassuring messages about the validity of the content and that the publication does help fight crime.

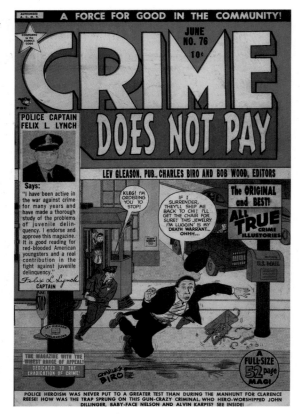

▼ In the feature story of *Crime Does Not Pay*, the character Mr. Crime would comment to the reader on the things that were happening, but he was never seen by the characters in the story. Mr. Crime would represent the criminals, but was always aware that "Crime Does Not Pay" (which, incidentally, was printed on top of every page, in case anyone would forget).

In the early heyday of the booming American comic book industry, publishers were always looking for new titles to supply to the voracious, ever-expanding market. After superheroes, crime became the next big thing, following hot on the heels of an array of very successful crime magazines. The magazines, in their turn, were inspired by the visibility of crime in American society, with notorious gangsters, hold-ups, and murders reported daily in every newspaper.

The comic book that launched this whole trend was *Crime Does Not Pay*, which was started in 1942 by the publisher Lev Gleason. The inspiration came from Metro-Goldwyn-Mayer's very successful docudrama movie series of the same name from the mid-1930s (which, by the way, was endorsed by J. Edgar Hoover). The two editors, Charles Biro and Bob Wood, saw an opportunity to tap into a never-ending supply of stories to entertain and enthrall the readers and at the same time pose as guardians of moral values. All of this was accomplished with *Crime Does Not Pay*, since the stories were based on actual events and always ended with the criminals getting their righteous punishment. Under this guise of moral docudrama, Biro and Wood got away with murder.

▲ The publisher of *Crime Does Not Pay* once advertised that they had six million readers, figuring that every copy of the one million they sold every month was read by at least six people. Looking at this old, battered, and loved comic book from 1947, it is easy to believe that their statement was true.

The success was immediate. The first couple of issues sold around 200,000 copies each. In 1946 that figure rose to 800,000, and by 1948 sales were averaging one million copies each month. At this time the publisher had started to print the incredible boast, "More than 6,000,000 Readers Monthly," a figure based on reader surveys that showed that several people read each copy sold. This made the other publishers take notice, and soon the market was flooded with copycats. More than forty comic book publishers—that is, just about everyone in the business—published 150 crime titles during the next decade, making crime one of the best-selling comics genres ever.

It is quite clear that these comics were a response to the postwar appetite for realistic and action-packed entertainment, but the question remains as to whether they actually conveyed a message that prevented crime. Many of the titles that followed *Crime Does Not Pay* were not as diligent as the editors of that comic in making sure that the message was, indeed, "crime does not pay." And it is quite likely that many of the readers reveled in the events depicted and might even have identified with the criminals.

One source of information is the comic book's letters page, which is full of testimonials of the crime-preventing effect it had. Children, parents, teachers, police officers, and former criminals all wrote and assured that reading *Crime Does Not Pay* had helped them in some way to see the light and step away from a career of crime. That the comic book offered a reward of two dollars for every printed letter probably had something to do with this seemingly endless stream of praise from the readers.

Whether the publishers actually wanted to prevent crime, or just sell more copies of their comic books, we will never know, although it is an essential question in ascertaining if these crime comics were in fact propaganda or not. What is quite certain is that they did have an impact on a whole generation of American readers.

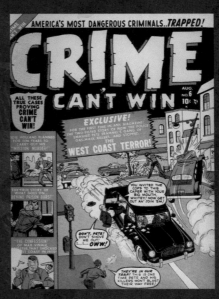

◄ *Crime Can't Win* was one of the hundreds of imitators of *Crime Does Not Pay* that were issued by almost every comics publisher in the U.S. after WWII, when superhero comics went out of fashion.

▼ The endings of the American crime stories of the 1940s and 1950s were always the same: the criminal was caught and punished according to his crime. Here is a scene from the comic book *Crime and Justice* from 1954, in which a thief is not only shot when trying to escape, but also humiliated when he is made to realize that the money he tried to steal was worthless.

Seduction of the Innocent!

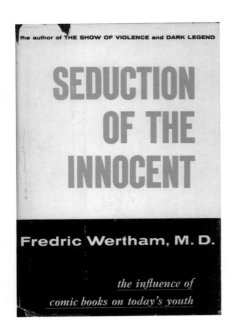

◄ ◄ *Seduction of the Innocent: The Influence of Comic Books on Today's Youth*, **was published in 1954 and immediately started an avalanche of criticism aimed at the comic book industry.**

◄ **One of many illustrations that were included in the image section in the middle of Wertham's book. All illustrations in** *Seduction of the Innocent* **had captions containing sardonic comments by Wertham. This image had the caption, "A sample of the injury-to-the-eye motif."**

The most all-encompassing and thoroughly effective propaganda campaign in the field of comics was not with, through, or even for comics—it was against the medium altogether. When Fredric Wertham, a highly distinguished psychologist, released his book *Seduction of the Innocent* in 1954, it started a veritable witch hunt on comics all around the world.

But the campaign against comics did not start with *Seduction of the Innocent*, however. As early as 1940, when comic books were still a rather new phenomenon, the *National Education Association Journal* ran an article with the rather self-explanatory title "An Antidote to the Comic Magazine Poison." Dr. Wertham found comic books in the course of his work with juvenile offenders, and noted that many of the delinquents read comics avidly, concluding, perhaps too hastily, that they were important environmental factors leading these kids to a life of crime and violence. He first presented his thoughts in an article published in 1947, and after that he

embarked on a crusade against violent comic books. Over the course of the following years, he would give lectures and write articles, so that when *Seduction of the Innocent* was published in 1954, it was the spark that lit this already overflowing powder keg, just waiting to explode. And explode it did.

Seduction of the Innocent caused alarm among parents and gave them the reason they needed to campaign for censorship through PTAs, church groups, mothers' clubs, and other organizations. Journalists picked up on the theme and pretty soon everyone was condemning comics, right and left. What Wertham stated in his book was that comic books were a dangerous form of popular literature and a serious cause of crime and illiteracy among youths in the U.S. Wertham cited numerous depictions of violence, sex, drug abuse, and other adult themes within "crime comics"—a term he used to describe not only the popular crime-oriented titles of the time (the kind discussed on

In ordinary comic books, there are pictures within pictures for children who know how to look.

◀◀ When doing research for *Seduction of the Innocent*, Wertham really did look long and hard at comics. So is this the result of a cartoonist trying to pervert the minds of the young readers, or the delusions of an already perverted mind? You decide.

◀ The trials and tribulations of comics did not end with Wertham. In Great Britain, a trial was held in 1973 to try to prove that the content of the British comic book *Nasty Tales* was obscene. When the verdict fell as not guilty, the publisher issued a "Trial Special" with court transcripts redone as comics. Here Martin Sudden's version of a part in the defense's closing statement.

the previous pages), but also superhero, fantasy, and horror comics. From this Wertham asserted—largely based on undocumented and unverified anecdotes—that reading comics encouraged children to mimic these behaviors and use drugs or resort to violence.

If anyone was ever in doubt that Wertham was out to get comics, this line from *Seduction of the Innocent* should suffice to convince: "The difference between surreptitious pornographic literature for adults and children's comic books is this: in one it is a question of attracting perverts, in the other of making them."

The effects were severe and are still felt today, half a century later. Generations of teachers, librarians, and parents were convinced that Wertham was right, and they more or less banned comics in schools and libraries. PTA groups made sure that comics were taken off the shelves of the local stores, while censorship through the Comics

Code Authority saw to it that only the blandest comics were allowed to survive. All of this caused the development of comics as an art form to be thrown back several decades.

Wertham himself was proud of what he had achieved. He wrote in his later book *The Sign of Cain*, published in 1966: "When *Seduction of the Innocent* appeared in the middle fifties, it started a grass-roots social reaction . . . A change occurred. Murder in comic books decreased, and so did the number of crime-comic-book publishers. Within a few years after the publication of *Seduction of the Innocent*, twenty-four out of twenty-nine crime-comic-book publishers went out of business."

Late in his career, Wertham repented and admitted that comic readers might not have turned out so bad in his last book *The World of Fanzines* from 1974, but by then it was all too late and other forces in society had taken his ideas to heart.

▲ A photo of the (in comics circles) infamous Dr. Wertham, reading one of the very comic books he was about to put out of business: *Shock SuspenStories*.

Self-Regulation: The Proven Solution?

THE FINISHED STORY IS THEN PROOF-READ AND SENT TO THE COMICS CODE AUTHORITY FOR REVIEW AND APPROVAL.

◄◄ The seal of approval that all American comic books needed to have on their covers in order to get distribution. Without it, almost no distributor would touch the book, and it would get returned in unopened packages.

◄ Here's how the Comics Code Authority thought it should work. Within a two-page comic, telling readers about the process of creating a comic book, was this panel showing how easy it was to get the approval of comics from the Comics Code Authority.

Code for Editorial Matter

General Standards: Part A

(1) Crimes shall never be presented in such a way as to create sympathy for the criminal, to promote distrust of the forces of law and justice, or to inspire others with a desire to imitate criminals.

(2) No comics shall explicitly present the unique details and methods of a crime.

(3) Policemen, judges, Government officials, and respected institutions shall never be presented in such a way as to create disrespect for established authority.

(4) If crime is depicted it shall be as a sordid and unpleasant activity.

(5) Criminals shall not be presented so as to be rendered glamorous or to occupy a position which creates a desire for emulation.

(6) In every instance good shall triumph over evil and the criminal punished for his misdeeds.

(7) Scenes of excessive violence shall be prohibited. Scenes of brutal torture, excessive and unnecessary knife and gunplay, physical agony, gory and gruesome crime shall be eliminated.

(8) No unique or unusual methods of concealing weapons shall be shown.

(9) Instances of law-enforcement officers dying as a result of a criminal's activities should be discouraged.

(10) The crime of kidnapping shall never be portrayed in any detail, nor shall any profit accrue to the abductor or kidnaper. The criminal or the kidnaper must be punished in every case.

(11) The letters of the word "crime" on a comics-magazine cover shall never be appreciably greater in dimension than the other words contained in the title. The word "crime" shall never appear alone on a cover.

(12) Restraint in the use of the word "crime" in titles or subtitles shall be exercised.

General Standards: Part B

(1) No comic magazine shall use the word horror or terror in its title.

(2) All scenes of horror, excessive bloodshed, gory or gruesome crimes, depravity, lust, sadism, masochism shall not be permitted.

(3) All lurid, unsavory, gruesome illustrations shall be eliminated.

(4) Inclusion of stories dealing with evil shall be used or shall be published only where the intent is to illustrate a moral issue and in no case shall evil be presented alluringly, nor so as to injure the sensibilities of the reader.

(5) Scenes dealing with, or instruments associated with walking dead, torture, vampires and vampirism, ghouls, cannibalism, and werewolfism are prohibited.

General Standards: Part C

All elements or techniques not specifically mentioned herein, but which are contrary to the spirit and intent of the code, and are considered violations of good taste or decency, shall be prohibited.

Dialogue

(1) Profanity, obscenity, smut, vulgarity, or words or symbols which have acquired undesirable meanings are forbidden.

(2) Special precautions to avoid references to physical afflictions or deformities shall be taken.

(3) Although slang and colloquialisms are acceptable, excessive use should be discouraged and, wherever possible, good grammar shall be employed.

Religion

(1) Ridicule or attack on any religious or racial group is never permissible.

Costume

(1) Nudity in any form is prohibited, as is indecent or undue exposure.

(2) Suggestive and salacious illustration or suggestive posture is unacceptable.

(3) All characters shall be depicted in dress reasonably acceptable to society.

(4) Females shall be drawn realistically without exaggeration of any physical qualities.

NOTE: It should be recognized that all prohibitions dealing with costume, dialogue, or artwork applies as specifically to the cover of a comic magazine as they do to the contents.

Marriage and sex

(1) Divorce shall not be treated humorously nor represented as desirable.

(2) Illicit sex relations are neither to be hinted at nor portrayed. Violent love scenes as well as sexual abnormalities are unacceptable.

(3) Respect for parents, the moral code, and for honorable behavior shall be fostered. A sympathetic understanding of the problems of love is not a license for morbid distortion.

(4) The treatment of live-romance stories shall emphasize the value of the home and the sanctity of marriage.

(5) Passion or romantic interest shall never be treated in such a way as to stimulate the lower and baser emotions.

(6) Seduction and rape shall never be shown or suggested.

(7) Sex perversion or any inference to same is strictly forbidden.

In the middle of the 1950s, the attacks against comics were reaching a fever pitch. Self-proclaimed guardians of American public morality mounted numerous campaigns against comic books. In response to these threats, several of the major comic book publishers banded together to start a self-censoring system: the Comics Code Authority.

The approval of the Comics Code was soon established as mandatory, and comic books published without the seal of approval of the Code were not handled by the distributors. The outward raison d'être for the Comics Code was to eliminate all things that were deemed unsavory and reestablish trust in the public's eye for comic books. Looking through the original regulations (which can be found in the box opposite), it is obvious that what the group establishing these rules had in mind was much more than that.

For instance, the section about marriage and sex may very well have been in line with what the general public in the U.S. thought in the 1950s, but reading it today it does sound like something dictated by the Church, using comics as tools of propaganda to send out messages of what is good and what is bad. Seeing that the President of the Comics Magazine Association of America—which was the group overseeing the Comics Code—John L. Goldwater was also the chief editor for Archie Comics, which did license *Archie* for evangelical Christian messages (see the chapter Religious Rants), this does not sound altogether impossible (even if Goldwater himself was Jewish). If you

still think this is stretching it a bit, consider the following statement by Goldwater from the 1964 book *Americana in Four Colors*: ". . . it is not an over-statement to say that the influence for good exerted by the program has had considerable social significance, reaching far beyond the industry it has regulated."

Another reflection is that the rules under *General Standards: Part B* seem to have been written more or less directly to put Entertaining Comics (EC) out of business. EC was the most successful publisher of comic books with stories about crime, horror, science fiction, and war, something that naturally irked the other publishers. The publisher of EC, William Gaines, did try to conform to the regulations, but the Code's reactionary ideas made for a short-lived relationship. The final straw was *Judgment Day*—the story of an astronaut who visits a planet of orange and blue robots. He witnesses the robots' mutual prejudice and concludes that the planet is not ready for admission into the Galactic Empire. Returning home, the astronaut takes off his helmet to reveal himself as a black man. In 1956 the Code's censors decreed that the character could not be black. No amount of persuasion and assurances that the whole idea of this anti-racist story was dependent on the fact that the character was black helped. EC finally published the story without any changes after having threatened to otherwise make the whole affair public, but ultimately all of the comic books published by EC, except *MAD Magazine*, were canceled, and the other publishers got rid of their competitor.

▶ The cover of one of the issues that were debated in the infamous Kefauer Hearing. Publisher Bill Gaines thought this was "in good taste," since he had managed to have the cartoonist Johnny Craig lower the image, so that the blood-dripping neck was not revealed. The Senate Subcommittee investigator did not agree.

◀ The famous last part of the comic *Judgment Day*, where the representatives of the Comics Code Authority said that the character was not allowed to be black. Since the story was published in the very last issue of *Weird Science*, which was canceled along with almost all the other titles from EC due to the regulations of the Code, publisher Bill Gaines probably felt that he could afford to go against the Comics Code Authority anyway.

Let's Go Shooting!

Comics have been used extensively to promote merchandise of all kinds, shapes, and forms. In the U.S., the major era for using comic books for this kind of advertising was the 1950s and 1960s. Most often, the messages of these comics are easy to detect and not especially provocative. And then there are the comic books produced for the gun manufacturer Remington . . .

There were at least two of these: *How to Shoot* from 1952 and *Let's Go Shooting* from 1956. They were promotional comic books, produced for and distributed through Remington Du Pont. This is made very clear, both overtly on the cover blurb stating, "Remington: Serving American Sportsmen since 1816," and in the ad on the back listing different gun models with the caption, "For a Lifetime of Shooting Fun;" but it's also done (slightly) more covertly, with the characters

saying things like "Just as I expected, Billy . . . Your New Remington is right on the nose!" with Bill responding "What Accuracy!"

The stories in these two books are fairly similar. In *Let's Go Shooting*, two children visit their uncle, an experienced hunter, who teaches them about hunting and gun safety. The gun safety parts seem pretty accurate and are presented in a didactic and convincing way, and could pass as educational and/or informational to most readers, even today. The other parts, however, are much more likely to be seen as propaganda. To start with we are presented with an older man who tries to convince two young people of the beauty of shooting and of owning a rifle. Doubtless for many Americans there is nothing strange about this, but for someone living outside the U.S., where rifles in most cases are something owned only by

◄ *Let's Go Shooting* and *How to Shoot* were two educational comic books produced for the gun manufacturer Remington in the 1950s. Their clear aim was to get young kids, especially boys, interested in shooting and using a Remington.

GUN CAN BE
U A LOT OF PLEASURE, TOO.
TO TOWN AND YOU CAN
PICK OUT A RIFLE.

Background illustration
Here is a statement
that pretty much sums up
the message of *Let's Go*
Shooting. Using a gun can
be both useful and "give
you a lot of pleasure."

professional hunters or people in the military,
it does sound rather odd to try to convince
youngsters of wanting to own a potentially
lethal weapon.

Another part that makes these comics seem very
dated is that although they both have boys and
girls in the stories, presumably to make sure that
readers of both sexes feel included, the focus is
very obviously on the boys. The girls are there
as giggling hang-arounds, who are lent the boys'
rifles but not given one of their own, and they are
always ready to cheer the boys on. This is very
indicative of the 1950s, and can also be seen as a
kind of propaganda, a message and a wish for the
preservation of things as they are, with the women
being there to support the men, always taking
second place and not getting in the way. More
about this later, in the chapter Sexual Slander.

Back to the question of using rifles. There are
always two sides to an argument, and not everyone
agrees that animals are perfect for shooting practice.
In the comic book *Born to Be Wild*, published in 1991
for the benefit of P.E.T.A. (People for the Ethical
Treatment of Animals), a host of the most famous
(mostly) American cartoonists of the era contributed
comics for the cause. Among these were Neil
Gaiman (*Sandman*), Todd McFarlane (*Spawn*),
Moebius (*The Airtight Garage*), Grant Morrison
(*The Invisibles*, *New X-Men*, *Batman*), and Peter
Kuper (*World War 3*).

The comics in *Born to Be Wild* mostly argue against
animal testing in laboratories, often using allegories
to make the reader understand what we are doing
to these animals. Some of them are really effective,
hitting the reader just as hard as young Bill did the
coyote on the cover of *Let's Go Shooting*.

► The very first scene
from *Let's Go Shooting*.
Here we see the two clean
cut and very American
youngsters, Bill and Judy,
visiting Uncle Fred at the
"Gun Smoke Lodge,"
complete with all kinds of
shooting trophies. Notice
that Bill is going to get
educated in the ways of
firearms, and that ". . .
we'll even teach Judy a
thing or two." Her reaction,
"Oh boy!" just about
says it all.

►► A message from "the
other side." In the story
Babycakes, from the comic
book *Born to Be Wild*, Neil
Gaiman and Michael Zulli
tell the story of what would
happen if all the animals
on our planet disappeared,
showing that we would use
babies as a substitute. A
powerful allegory that
makes the reader think
about what we put
animals through.

▼ **Raeburn Van Buren contributed to** *It's Fun to Stay Alive* **with a single panel, featuring the characters from his comic strip** *Abbie an' Slats*.

This comic was started and written by Al Capp, of *Li'l Abner* **fame, but in 1948 he had left the strip, and this panel is signed only by Van Buren.**

▼ *Bugs Bunny, of all irresponsible, extroverted characters, teaches Daffy Duck and the other Warner Brothers characters about safety and responsible*

behavior in traffic. This comic is not signed, but could have been done by Chase Craig.

ABBIE AN' SLATS   **By VAN BUREN**

YOU'RE A GOOD DRIVER, BATHLESS!

KEERECT, ABBIE! I FIGGERS THAT CAREFUL DRIVIN' IS THE BEST CAR AND LIFE INSURANCE IN THE WORLD!

SHOWING OFF ON A BIKE MAY LOOK GAY ... BUT KIDS OFTEN GET HURT IN THAT WAY...

GREEN IS NOT RED AND RED IS NOT GREEN ... STUDY THE LIGHTS SO YOU'LL KNOW WHAT THEY MEAN!

THAT'S ALL FOR TODAY- BUT REMEMBER TO SAY: 'IT'S BETTER TO BE SAFE THAN SORRY!

I'M NOT GOING TO CROSS IN THE MIDDLE OF THE BLOCK ANY MORE!

--AND NO MORE TRICKS ON MY BIKE FOR ME!!

© COURTESY OF WARNER BROS CARTOONS

► *Henry* **was one of the more successful comic strips included in** *It's Fun to Stay Alive*. **It was made by Carl Anderson in 1946, according to the copyright note, two years before he died. The comic strip was a pantomime, which is why the teachings of this panel are shown in a rhymed caption, something that may have felt antiquated even in 1948.**

►► **When first glancing through** *It's Fun to Stay Alive*, **one might be tricked into believing that the great Milton Caniff contributed to the project, but this page is actually signed Ray Bailey, who was a former assistant to Caniff.**

HENRY   **By CARL ANDERSON**

ALL LITTLE KIDS WHO PLAY IN THE STREET SOONER OR LATER GET KNOCKED OFF THEIR FEET!

SIGNT= HENRY

CARL ANDERSON

BRUCE GENTRY by RAY BAILEY

NOW THAT I'M OLD ENOUGH T' DRIVE, HOW ABOUT A COUPLA TIPS, BRUCE?

CHICK, YOU'VE GOT TO BE AS ALERT DRIVING AT NIGHT AS FLYING AT NIGHT...

HUH? AW! YOU'RE KIDDIN'!

NO, I'M NOT! THE SAFETY FACTORS ALL IMPORTANT IN EACH...IN DRIVING, REMEMBER TO: 1. GO SLOW ON WET PAVEMENT

2. DON'T OVER-DRIVE HEADLIGHTS... 3. SLOW DOWN AT INTERSECTIONS...

YIPE! I SEE WHAT I MEAN?

4. KEEP YOUR LIGHTS AND BRAKES IN CONDITION...5. DON'T FOLLOW THE CAR AHEAD TOO CLOSE...

WHAT WERE YOU SAYIN' ABOUT FLARES, BRUCE?

THEY HAVE THEIR PLACE IN NIGHT FLYING AND NIGHT DRIVING... MORE FOLKS SHOULD FOLLOW THE EXAMPLE OF TRUCK DRIVERS IN USE OF FLARES WHEN CARS STALL...

It's Fun to Stay Alive

▶ One of my all-time favorite titles to an educational/informational comic book. On the surface it told readers about traffic safety measures, but in the process all kids reading it would be persuaded by these auto sellers that cars are an essential part of life.

Comics can be used in many different ways and for many different purposes, as should be evident from the examples in this book. Over the years, many people have used comic books as a way to inform the general public of things that the creator, publisher, or sponsor deemed important to inform/indoctrinate. Whether these comic books are educational, informational, or propaganda is of course in the eye of the beholder.

The comic book *It's Fun to Stay Alive*, from 1948, has one of the best titles ever given to an educational/informational pamphlet. Here's the purpose of this sixteen-page giveaway comic, as spelled out on its inside-back-cover: "*It's Fun to Stay Alive* is a public service project of The Ohio Automobile Dealers Association in co-operation with America's leading cartoonists and their syndicates."

Well, "America's leading cartoonists" is stretching it . . . The artists featured are mostly second-string, at best. But that only makes this little giveaway comic even more interesting. The content is short comics, evidently made especially for *It's Fun to Stay Alive*, which showcase easy-to-understand safety lessons delivered by more or less famous "stars" of comic strips from the time. These include *Henry* by Carl Anderson, *The Toodles* by Rod and Ruth Baer (signed as "Rod Ruth"), *Bruce Gentry* by Ray Bailey, *The Berrys* by Carl Grubert, *Bugs Bunny* (possibly by Chase Craig), *Tim Tyler* by Lyman Young, *Elmer* by "Doc" Winner, *Joe Jinks* by Henry Formhals, *Abbie an' Slats* by Raeburn Van Buren, *Dixie Dugan* by McEvoy and John H. Striebe, and *Cokey* by Duane Bryers.

So, not the "best and the brightest" perhaps, but all very indicative of the time in which this comic book was produced. It really feels like something out of another era when you are asked to wait for the policeman to blow his whistle before crossing an intersection, or told that waving with your hand outside of the window is not an acceptable signal for making a turn with your car. Mostly, though, the advice seems sound enough, even by today's standards. Traffic hasn't changed all that much.

OK, so where's the propaganda, you may ask? Well, there need not be any sinister plan behind the information transmitted for something to be deemed propaganda. In this case, the intent of teaching kids about safety in traffic might seem entirely informational and "safe." The fact that *It's Fun to Stay Alive* was produced by an association of auto-dealers who were selling the very instruments with which, in the words of the pamphlet itself, "Nearly one out of three accidental deaths of school-age children results from," is probably proof enough that there might be an underlying message. Maybe the association of auto-dealers wanted to have something to show when confronted with the ghastly figures of the consequences of using cars in society. Or, if you are looking for a more sinister scheme behind this, the whole idea might have been to transmit the message that we need cars in order to live, or at least to feel alive. In the U.S. at the time, post-World War II, this was a "truth" that didn't really need any propaganda to help it along, but today with global warming, holes in the ozone layer, and so on, the messages of the car dealers becomes painfully evident.

Camel: First in the Service!

One of the most common misconceptions about comics is that they represent a way of communication solely geared towards young readers. True, there are a lot of comics made for children all over the world, but that does not mean that comics should be used to entertain children exclusively—something a quick look through the graphic novels section of any book store might show you. Comics are an art form like any other, and can thus be used to do just about anything the artist and writer can imagine. Still, a lot of people around the world perpetuate this misunderstanding, even today, and often react when something they do not deem suitable for children is displayed in a comic, no matter if it was originally created for children or for adults.

This was not always the case, however. There was a time when comics were just as much for adults as for children, maybe even more so. This was when the majority of comics were printed in daily or weekly newspapers, which had mostly adult readers. The arrival of comic books changed all that, quickly establishing children as the main audience and slowly changing the public's opinion of what comics were supposed to be all about. But before this change, there were often advertisers using the form of comics to sell things that were not for children at all.

To be truthful, there were comics ads selling just about everything, including a lot of pretty harmless things, like Kellogg's Corn Flakes, Aunt Jemina's pancakes, or the caffeine-free Postum, which was sometimes marketed by an invisible cartoon ghost named "Mister Coffee Nerves." Another example was *Pepsi and Pete, the Pepsi Cola Cops*, drawn by none other then Rube Goldberg. But there were other ads that would stand out as unsuitable today. For example, a lot of specially designed comics advertised various brands of cigarettes. The brand Kool had comics ads featuring a cute little penguin called Willie that by today's standard really would be deemed too heavily geared towards young readers. They were published into the 1950s,

when the debate about comics probably made the medium an unsuitable vehicle for any kind of advertising. Philippe Morris had comics ads, also in the 1950s, with the characters from the very popular TV show *I Love Lucy*, making sure that the readers knew what the stars of the show smoked. Frank Robbins, who was most famous for doing the strip *Johnny Hazzard*, also did comics ads for Bond Street tobacco.

One of the most fervent users of comics in their ads was Camel. These are particularly noteworthy during the early years of the 1940s. Due to World War II, the content shifted from movie stars and athletes to focussing on male servicemen and female war workers. Reading these ads today, they are, despite what they try to achieve, very charming. They consist of two comic strips, mostly telling the stories of servicemen having small adventures, always leading up to the payoff—relaxing after whatever had happened invariably involved smoking a Camel cigarette.

The ads always showed a beautiful woman at the bottom, holding a cigarette and exclaiming in a word balloon that she preferred Camels as they were ". . . fresh and flavorful and don't get my throat." They also displayed a curious box with a woman with a "T" over parts of her face, claiming that it was "in the T-zone where cigarettes are judged." The image looks remarkably like later non-smoking ads, showing where the negative results of smoking hit.

▶ This comics ad for Camel from 1944 shows Marianne de Sydow, a skiing star of the time. Notice the photo used to establish that this actually is the ski star in question. Today, no professional athlete would advertise tobacco, but in the 1940s this was not uncommon.

▲◄ Here we see Jane Harmond, billed as a war worker at Autoflight Corp. (the women in these ads were all war workers during WWII), selling us Camels because of their "fresh appeal" and the fact that they are "easy on her throat." Also notice the advert for the "T-zone," a mainstay in ads for Camel in the 1940s.

▲ Another example of a comics ad for Camel from 1944. Here the cool pilots show just how they keep their cool.

◄ Another beautiful comics ad from the war years showing us that even female recruits smoke Camel. The slogan "First in the Service" was used all through WWII, being based on supposed actual sales records for servicemen.

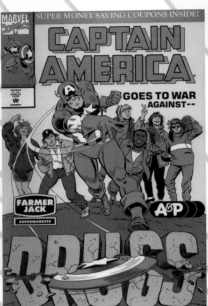

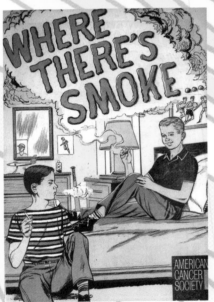

►► One of the most talked about anti-drugs comics ever was published in the political run of *Green Lantern/Green Arrow* in 1971. Dennis O'Neil and Neal Adams took on some really heavy subjects, like racism, poverty, and drug abuse. Here a pivotal scene from the story "They Say It'll Kill Me . . . But They Won't Say When!"

◄ An example of an anti-drugs comic from the 1990s (1992 to be exact), written by Peter David and drawn by Sal Veluto and Keith Williams. Inside is the same story that has been done over and over again, about the athlete who tries drugs to get away from the pressure, but sees the right way when helped along by a man in spandex.

◄ This informational comic book was published by the American Cancer Society in 1965. The message of non-smoking is presented here by an expert at the American Cancer Society to a visiting family with a young son who has just been caught smoking his first cigarette. The overtly didactic story probably didn't convince many of the dangers of smoking, to say nothing about the happy faces of the first time smokers on the cover.

► An illustration from the special edition of *The New Teen Titans* from 1983, produced "in cooperation with the President's drug awareness campaign." In 1983 that meant Ronald Reagan, and this comic book has a letter signed by Nancy Reagan on the inside cover.

Where There's Smoke . . .

When examining old comics, especially comics from the first part of the twentieth century, you'll have no problem finding characters that smoke. Almost everyone did. Jiggs in *Bringing up Father* did. The dad in *Dennis the Menace* did. The cowboy *Lucky Luke* did (until the publishers had him stop and start chewing on a straw instead). Dagwood in *Blondie* did. Captain Easy did in *Wash Tubs and Captain Easy*. Popeye smoked a corn-pipe in *Thimble Theatre*. The Dragon Lady in *Terry and the Pirates* smoked cigarettes in long thin holders. Almost everyone smoked at one time or another. So, finding comics characters "advertising" the habit of smoking is no problem. But comics have also been used to try to convince people not to smoke, both ordinary cigarettes and heavier stuff.

In the 1950s and 1960s, you could get giveaway comics with rather obvious, and not always very convincing stories about the dangers of smoking and/or drug abuse. Good examples of this are the comics for the American Cancer Society. In 1965 it issued the comic *Where There's Smoke . . .*, with a story about a boy who is caught smoking and is taken by his parents to the American Cancer Society and told all the horrible facts about smoking by an expert. Not very convincing, but still, perhaps more effective than just having these facts presented as diagrams and curves. When looking at another comic book by the same institute, *Taking a Chance . . . with No Chance to Win* from 1976, it soon becomes evident that the cartoonist has started out with the same script and adjusted it to the 1970s. Gone is the secure family of the 1960s, and instead we here follow a cool set of friends discussing the habit of smoking. But they still end up with an expert from the American Cancer Society (albeit a much more hip expert with big blond hair and massive seventies glasses), telling them exactly the same things. Both comics are, it has to be said, pretty boring to read.

Another from this period is a comic book called *Trapped!*, from 1951. It tells the story of a regular guy (they are always regular guys in these stories) who slowly but surely gets dragged into drug abuse by first trying a "reefer." When addiction gets a hold of him, he turns to harder drugs and finally gets mixed up with crime and ends up in jail, where his best friend hangs himself. This is a well told, evocative story and a good read, and one which just might have turned a few young Americans away from thoughts of trying drugs.

Later on, superheroes were enlisted in the fight against drugs. There is more to come later in this chapter on Stan Lee's use of Spider-Man as an anti-drugs icon in the early 1970s, but he was not alone. One of the most famous anti-drugs stories in comics was printed in the superhero comic book *Green Lantern/Green Arrow* in 1971. The writer Dennis O'Neil had Green Arrow's young sidekick (aptly named Speedy) become a drug addict, and the story was so moving that the Mayor of New York City wrote a letter to the publisher commending their contribution to the war on drugs.

In the 1980s, the heroes for young readers were the stars of *The New Teen Titans*, and they were subsequently drafted into the drug war with a special comic book made in cooperation with President Reagan's Drug Awareness Campaign. This was written by Marv Wolfman, an experienced scriptwriter, and had the same basic story as *Trapped!* only turned just a little bit silly by having superheroes running around trying to stop things.

In the 1990s, Captain America and Spider-Man took turns fighting drug in the comic books *Captain America Goes to War Against Drugs* and *The Amazing Spider-Man: Skating on Thin Ice*. Both these comics contain the same story: an athlete tempted to try drugs to wind down ends up being rescued by the costume-clad hero of the day.

All of these examples show that comics have been continuously used to fight smoking and drug abuse, and they also show how the cartoonists have adjusted to the changing times in their efforts to reach young readers.

From Freak Brothers to Cocaine Comix

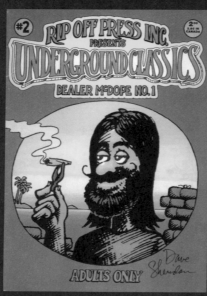

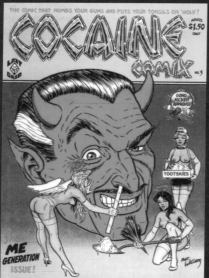

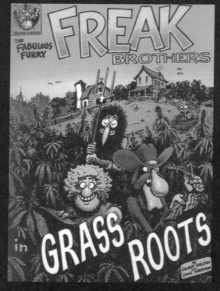

◄◄ The third issue of *Cocaine Comix* from 1981. By the time of the last issue, published in 1984, the problems associated with cocaine had become so evident that the dismissive and/or even positive attitude in the comics had changed to being more cautiously against drugs.

◄ *The Fabulous Furry Freak Brothers* by Gilbert Shelton, the first and foremost proponents of drug use in comics. Shelton has produced thirteen issues of the title since its inception three decades ago, and they have all been kept in print since then.

◄◄◄ *Dopin' Dan* by Ted Richards from 1973. This comic book, which lasted four issues between 1972 and 1981, did include scenes with the use of readily available drugs in a foreign country, but the main focus was making fun of the soldier's situation in Vietnam.

◄◄ *Dealer McDope* by Dave Sheridan. This is a reprint collection from 1985, with material from the early 1970s. Dealer McDope was used extensively as a symbol for the legalization of marijuana.

◄ An ad by Dave Sheridan, which was used in several election campaigns to decriminalize marijuana in California during the early 1970s. It is of course ironic to use the very same image that has been used to make people enlist in the army in the service of the hippie generation who fervently opposed the Vietnam War.

As seen on the previous pages, there has been no shortage of comics trying to persuade readers not to smoke, be it ordinary cigarettes or illegal substances. As is almost always the case, there are also comics advocating the exact opposite. When it comes to comics pushing the use of drugs, the underground period in American and British comics is the place to be.

The underground/hippie movement as a whole saw drugs as a way to finally free the human spirit and expand the mind. The drug of choice was marijuana—otherwise known as cannabis, pot, ganja, and an assortment of alternative names. This was a love affair that got started in the 1960s and went on into the 1970s, until the problems associated with the use of heavier drugs became too evident and most of the pro-drug comics disappeared.

In the heyday of the underground movement, there was no shortage of comics advocating the use of drugs, however. There was usually at least one story about drugs in each underground anthology, but there were also titles more or less directly devoted to drugs, like *Tooney Loons* and *Marijuana Melodies*, *Home Grown*, *Dope Comix*, or *Stoned Out Funnies*.

The most famous of all pro-drug comics is without any doubt *The Fabulous Furry Freak Brothers* by Gilbert Shelton. This hapless trio, always looking for new ways of scoring dope, getting laid, and avoiding work, is one of the few titles from the underground period to actually survive and gain a worldwide following. Shelton had his character Freewheelin' Franklin utter probably the most famous quote on drugs during the entire underground period: "Dope will get you through times of no money better than money will get you through times of no dope."

Dopin' Dan was another drug icon of this era, written and drawn by Ted Richards. He was a recruit in the U.S. Army, sent to Vietnam and trying to make the best of the situation. Despite the title of the comic book, the stories did not always center on drugs, even though Dan did use dope from time to time. The name was actually more of a satirical play of the names of two famous comic strips of the time, *Sad Sack* and *Beatle Bailey*, both featuring more sanitized versions of the life of a recruit in the army.

A third drug icon was *Dealer McDope*—the creation of cartoonist Dave Sheridan—described as the quintessential marijuana merchant. His stories were published in various comic books between 1969 and 1976, and also used as the poster image for the campaign to legalize marijuana in California in 1972 (with an astounding 34% of the vote in favor of the proposition).

As the times went by, the underground movement . . . well, moved on, and most of the comics of this era vanished. Others took their place, and reflected the new harsher times, like *Cocaine Comix*, launched in 1976, or *Harold Hedd in Hitler's Cocaine* from 1984. In Britain, the major advocate of drugs in comics during the underground period was without any doubt Bryan Talbot, who did numerous stories with his character Chester P. Hackenbush, the Psychedelic Alchemist. In more recent years, the anthology magazine *Northern Lightz*, containing comics with titles like *The Astounding Ganjaman*, *Spliff Warz*, *The Dopranos*, and *Great Moments in Dope History* has kept up the stoned tradition right through to today.

None of these comics—or comix as they were mostly called to distinguish them from the more traditional comic books—were carried by major distributors or sold by mainstream retail outlets. That does not mean that they didn't sell well, which they did, or didn't reach and affect large groups of readers. The funny, provocative dope comix of the underground may well have done much more to spread the idea of using drugs to free your mind than all the boring and overly pedagogic anti-drugs comics ever could hope of reversing.

▲ The groundbreaking issues of *Amazing Spider-Man*, published in 1971 in direct defiance of the Comics Code Authority. The popularity of these controversial comics paved the way for a more liberal approach to what could be written and drawn in an American comic book.

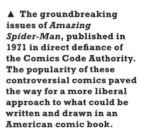

Spider-Man and the U.S. Department of Health

◄ This page shows in clear and evocative graphic storytelling how a person will succumb to the seductive powers of a drug dealer. Stan Lee and Gil Kane knew what they were doing.

Background illustration Harry Osborn falls for the allure of drugs, hoping that they will solve all his problems.

◄ Harry Osborn, a friend of Peter Parker and the son of the super-villain Green Goblin, has a nervous breakdown due to the abuse of illegal drugs. This panel is among the most beautiful and haunting representations of drug abuse ever made. Kids growing up in the 1970s will undoubtedly still recognize this panel on sight, as it stirred the emotions of large numbers of readers at the time.

In the midst of the political and social upheaval of the early 1970s, American comics changed. The comics business had for a long time been cowed into submission by the rules and regulations of the Comics Code Authority—but new times demanded a new form of comics.

As outlined earlier, the Comics Code Authority (see pages 92–93) was a censorship institution, installed by the comics publishers themselves as a form of self-defense against the massive criticism of comics during the 1950s, and its rules allowed nothing that could be deemed "controversial." This meant just about everything, which is one of the reasons why a lot of the superhero comics of this era turned bland and silly. There was really nothing serious left to build a story upon anymore, so the scriptwriters turned to more frivolous themes like super babies or giant monkeys.

Stan Lee, the author responsible for the creation of many of the most well-known superheroes such as the Fantastic Four, the Hulk, Daredevil, and the X-Men, was in 1971 editor-in-chief of the publishing house Marvel, but still managed to write several of their most popular characters. Among them was Spider-Man, another hero created by Lee. The popularity of the comic book *Amazing Spider-Man* prompted representatives from the Department of Health, Education, and Welfare to write Lee a letter asking him to use the influence Spider-Man had on kids to educate them on the dangers of drugs.

Lee, being an excellent storyteller, immediately realized that a story containing too much preaching to the young readers would make them shy away from both story and message. Instead he seamlessly wove it into the ongoing story about Spider-Man, who at this point was battling a villain named the Green Goblin. The person falling into the clutches of drugs was the Goblin's son, Harry Osborn, who also happened to be Peter Parker's (a.k.a. Spider-Man's) roommate and friend.

All comics published by Marvel at this time sported the Seal of Approval of the Comics Code Authority, and Lee dutifully submitted this storyline to them as well. They refused to give their permission because it contained mentions of drugs, which was not allowed under any circumstance. After having pointed out to them that the story was anti-drugs and that it was in effect commissioned by the United States government, Lee decided to publish the issues, without the seal of approval, as *Amazing Spider-Man #96–#98*.

These comics were hugely popular with readers, parents, the government, the media, and just about everyone else. This ultimately made the regulations of the Comics Code Authority look rather foolish, and in the end it resulted in the rules being changed and also caused the grip of this censorship agency to slowly weaken.

Even today, the comics make powerful reading, and it is evident how well Lee and artist Gil Kane understood how to reach their audience and get the message across without letting them realize what was going on. Potent propaganda to be sure! We don't know the extent of its impact, but several testimonies to the influence these stories had on young readers in the early 1970s exist, some actually giving *Amazing Spider-Man* as the reason they steered clear of drugs.

All-Atomic Power?

One subject that has created quite a stir in many countries is the question of whether or not to use nuclear power as a source of energy. The people arguing for and against this sensitive problem often came from very different camps, and the debate could get very intense indeed.

Naturally this argument has also spilled over into comics. In the U.S., several comics were made in the 1960s, commissioned by different nuclear technology-using power companies, to promote the idea of a "clean" and efficient new source of energy. A great example is the comic book *Power for Progress* from 1969, produced for the Consumers Power Company. This story tries to present its information as fact, but it is blatantly propagandistic. We follow "the Science Club of the Adams Junior High School" making appropriate "Oohs!" and "Aahs!" as their Clark Kent-lookalike teacher shows them around a nuclear plant. The information person at the plant (who incidentally looks just like a Ken doll), presents all the "facts," sounding like he's a robot programmed at an amusement park. Not a very convincing defense of nuclear power.

So, over to the other side. A few years later we find *All-Atomic Comics*, written and drawn by Leonard Rifas and published in 1976. This is a comic book with an openly anti-nuclear theme. Rifas even states on the inside cover that he set out to make an unbiased book. However he soon found that all the arguments for nuclear power were already out there, sponsored by "multi-million advertising campaigns," but that the arguments against nuclear power had little or no backing to make them better heard.

Thus *All-Atomic Comics* is an all-out attack on nuclear power. Rifas cleverly uses a three-legged frog (which was actually found at the time in the vicinity of a nuclear plant, but dismissed as a freak of nature) as a spokesperson for the arguments against nuclear power, and an evil light bulb named Greedy Killerwatt as his "debatable" opponent. A funny comic book, which is pretty convincing with a set of footnotes

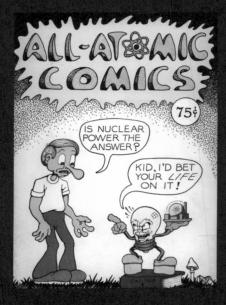

◄ *All-Atomic Comics* was written and drawn by Leonard Rifas and published by EduComics in 1976—a time when the debate over nuclear power was at its peak in many countries.

to substantiate its claims, but still of course a very biased presentation of the facts surrounding nuclear power.

Another example from this era is the book *Nuclear Power for Beginners*, by the British journalist and scriptwriter Stephen Croall and the cartoonist Kaianders Sempler, published in 1978. It is part of the *Beginners* book series, books that at least try to present their contents as unbiased facts. This particular book does nothing of the kind, however. Already on the first page you find reproductions of the famous 1970s button with a smiling sun and the text "Atomic Power—No Thanks!" in various versions from different European countries. The whole book is an attack on the powers in our society that hold nuclear energy to be a safe and sound alternative, and wraps up by listing all the other sources of energy available.

So where are we now in the discussion, over thirty years later? Well, considering that since then the character who has given a face to all the workers at nuclear power plants is the mumbling, stumbling Homer Simpson—I'd say that the opposition is ahead.

► Leonard Rifas goes all out in the use of allegorical imagery, as he has a mutated three-legged frog debate the pros and cons of nuclear power with an evil light bulb called "Greedy Killerwatt."

►► Presenting its content as information and facts only, the book *Nuclear Power for Beginners* was published in many countries during the heyday of the debate over nuclear power. This was not really unbiased, as the views presented were clearly stacked against nuclear power. This is the cover of the Swedish edition from 1979.

► *Power for Progress* was an "informational" comic book published in 1969 by the Consumers Power Company. I've put "informational" in quotation marks since this does imply some sort of unbiased view of things, which this comic book doesn't contain.

►► The final page of *Power for Progress*. Here the pro-nuclear preaching reaches new heights. The Clark Kent-lookalike is actually the teacher of a group of visiting students, but he seems to have been bribed by the Consumers Power Company.

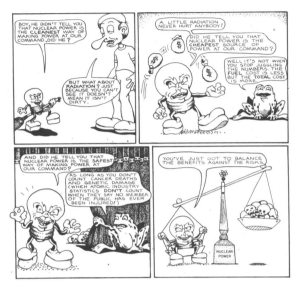

Chapter 5
Religious Rants

An example of a traditional
religious comic, re-imagining
a story from the Bible in comics
form. This page was taken from
the Catholic children's magazine
Treasure Chest of Fun and Facts.

Religion and Comics

▶ The first outright religious comic book ever published by the American superhero publisher Marvel Comics. *Francis, Brother of the Universe* was actually written by the Director of the Franciscan Communications office in New York, with the help of experienced people in the comics business like Mary Jo Duffy and John Buscema, but still, with a title like that, you do expect (and indeed get) quite a piece of propaganda.

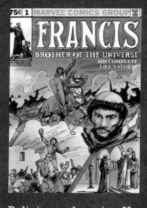

▲ A biography of a famous Russian ascetic and monk, who was made a Saint as late as 1987. The title, *Awaken Your Heart*, says it all. Interesting? Yes. Propaganda? Highly likely.

Religion and comics. Now there's another combination with the potential to raise an eyebrow or two. Some may see comics as too frivolous a medium to entrust with religious thoughts, or even that it would be demeaning to the message to convey it through comics. Others may see comics as too geared towards children, and thus not fit for any religious propaganda-like information that a child might have a problem understanding and evaluating properly. Either way, for many, comics are not a medium with which to entrust religious matters.

Even so, there is an abundance of comics with varying degrees of religious content. There are also, despite the righteous doubts just mentioned, examples of outright religious propaganda in comics. This is actually a rather common phenomenon, and throughout the years a large number of comics have been made to spread the "good" word. Those that I have come across—and will show in this chapter—are mostly Christian, but there are comics about all major religions, and more often than not the intent is clearly to "preach." These comics have been made by people set on convincing their fellow man of the "right" way of thinking, and prepared to utilize the accessibility, direct appeal, and impact that comics have to reach out and touch readers.

Most of these comics are rather easy to dismiss, as they almost always are made with a zeal to communicate "the message" that takes precedence over the ability to communicate, making them a

dreary read. They also have a habit of talking down to the reader in a way that can be quite annoying and off-putting to say the least. Comics readers used to the direct appeal of commercial comics would have little or no interest in these overly didactic efforts.

There are also the more subversive versions, with religious aspects woven into comics that on the surface deal with other things. These are not necessarily intentionally subversive, however. Religion is a part of many people's lives, including cartoonists', and that will influence the work they do. Still, having believable characters talk intelligently about religious thoughts and act out of religious beliefs can have a profound influence on the reader, without the cartoonist ever having had that in mind when he or she created the comics.

The distinction is, as ever, hard to make, and up to the reader to decide. For instance, was Charles Schulz's *Peanuts*, as has been argued in numerous books, a thoroughly Christian comic strip, or is this only due to Schulz's personal beliefs seeping through? (Or, indeed, is it simply a figment of the imagination of authors desperately wanting to ascribe aspects of their own religious beliefs to a popular phenomenon?)

Another example are the comics made by the French artist Joann Sfar, who is Jewish and more often than not has Jewish themes in his stories—like for instance in *Klezmer: Tales from the Wild East* or *The Rabbi's Cat*. These comics do not seem to have the intent to convert the readers to the Jewish faith (which is quite natural since Jews don't try to spread their religion to others through missionaries, etc.), and according to Sfar the Jewish themes are simply down to his own cultural inheritance. But there just might be an underlying thought of spreading an understanding of Jewish culture among the gentiles reading the comics.

Propaganda or not propaganda? I'll leave that to you to decide, as I will show a wide variety of religious comics in this chapter.

▲ A beautiful cover of an issue of Erik Larsen's comic book *The Savage Dragon*, from 1996. Here Larsen pokes fun at the superhero genre and lets loose the "ultimate battle of all times": God vs. the Devil.

◄ *The New Adventures of Jesus* by Frank Stack (a.k.a. Foolbert Sturgeon), from 1969. Stack worked under the name Foolbert Sturgeon to avoid persecution for his work while living in the Bible Belt, due to the fact that his stories about Jesus don't exactly conform to the traditional view of the Christian Messiah.

▲ The final scene from the comic *Chip Grant* by Griffin Jay and Ted Drake, taken from a 1953 issue of the magazine *The Catholic Boy*, which was published by the Holy Cross Fathers at the University of Notre Dame, Indiana. In this story, a student at a Catholic school gets beaten up for being an immigrant from behind the Iron Curtain, but the perpetrators are made to see the error of their ways. The scriptwriter manages to both attack Communism and show the true Catholic spirit of forgiveness in one fell swoop.

The World's Most Read . . . Comics?

The Bible is often described as the world's most read book. Its stories have been told in numerous ways and translated into numerous art forms, from oral stories by the fireside to full-length movies—and of course comics.

Many attempts have been made at conveying the stories from the Bible through comics, but most of these have been hampered by several, seemingly inherent, problems. One predicament is that many creators who have adapted the Bible into comics have had too much respect for the original texts and have tried to "include everything." The result is that they include all the action, but leave out the philosophical parts. In the case of the Bible, one of the world's most prominent philosophical and religious books, that is pretty inexcusable.

This respect may also produce stories that do not make use of comics' qualities as a visual medium, but rather use a restricted layout and design, almost as if doing it any differently would tarnish the stories contained within. This might also be a concession to ensure that as many readers as possible get the message. (A less forgiving interpretation is that the cartoonists involved are not always the best ones in the business.) No matter the reason, these comics often do not fully use the medium's potential to engage the reader, resulting in monotonous reading.

A bigger problem stems from the fact that many of the adaptations of the Bible were made by people who desperately wanted to convince the readers of the truths in the good book. This particular propagandistic goal has almost always resulted in comics that are as dull as doorknobs, making most intelligent readers quickly back away.

◄◄ A page from an adaption of Genesis, taken from the magazine *The Most Spectacular Stories Ever Told . . . from the Bible*. Notice the "superhuman" body of Adam and Eve, drawn by Joe Kubert, who is better known for drawing the war comics hero Sgt. Rock and the superhero Hawkman.

◄ In the graphic novel *Menneskesønnen (The Son of Man)* from 1995, the Danish cartoonist Peter Madsen has really thought about how to present the stories of The New Testament in a new and convincing way. This is the scene where Jesus is tempted by the Devil in the desert. The Devil is shown as a darker version of Jesus himself, with images portraying this scene as an inner struggle.

▶ A sample page from *Picture Stories from the Bible*, which shows just how tedious a read this can be. Trying to "blame" it on being from the 1940s does not work, since a lot of very compelling, moving comics were made at that time.

▶▶ *The Manga Bible* by British creators Siku and Akin was another attempt as late as 2007 to squeeze all the stories from the Bible into one volume of comics. Despite its modern appeal, this was another failure at doing justice to the stories in the Bible.

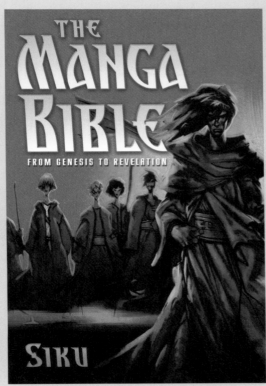

Examples of these dubious results are numerous. *Picture Stories from the Bible* from the mid-1940s, for instance, were pretty dull comics published by Educational Comics (later known as Entertaining Comics/EC, who in the 1950s were persecuted with a religious zeal). Perhaps if the very accomplished scriptwriters and cartoonists who worked for EC in its horror and crime comic heyday would have tackled the Bible, they could have given it some life, but alas that was not to be.

One step up in readability is *The Picture Bible* from around 1960, by Iva Hoth and Andre Le Blanc. These are some of the most widely spread Bible comics ever; they have been translated and sold in a number of countries all over the world and are still kept in print. Compared to *Picture Stories from the Bible*, these comics have a more compelling way of telling their stories—but they are still quite boring.

A more engaging effort can be found in the magazine *The Most Spectacular Stories Ever Told . . . from the Bible* from 1975, by Mayer, Kubert, and

Redondo. The images in these very American and bombastic comics suffer quite a lot from the fact that the people working on them usually drew action and superhero comics, but they are nevertheless a lot more entertaining than the above two mentioned adaptations.

More recent examples include *The Lion Graphic Bible* from 1998, by the British creators Mike Maddox and Jeff Anderson. This fully drawn version of the Bible also has the problem of trying to include just about everything between two covers and thus doesn't have enough space to flesh out each story properly. The same can be said about *The Manga Bible* from 2007, also made by two British creators, Siku and Akin Akinsiku, who tried to squeeze in the whole Bible in one go. No amount of manga styling could save this project, which, for instance, tried to sum up the whole *Book of Job* in one page.

Chick Tracts: Read Them or Be Damned!

THE CONTRACT! — HAPPY HALLOWEEN — THE ONLY HOPE — FATAL DECISION

THE MONSTER — THE BEAST — THE SCAM — ALLAH HAD NO SON

BIG DADDY? — NO FEAR? — A DEMON'S NIGHTMARE — BUSTED!

▲ A young kid, whose friend has just been killed, is told by a "caring" adult that he has gone to hell, despite the fact that he was a kind and generous person. From the tract *Happy Halloween*, designed especially for giving away to trick-or-treating kids.

▲ The way Jack T. Chick looks at his own creations. And with more than half a billion sold, he might not be all that wrong.

◄ **The so-called Chick Tracts have been published in one hundred different languages, and (according to the publisher) have sold more than five hundred million copies worldwide.**

The world's most enduring producer of propaganda comics is without any doubt the American Jack T. Chick. His so-called "Chick Tracts"—small pamphlets with comics made to convince readers to convert to the "true kind" of Christianity or spend the rest of eternity in hell—have been printed and sold in more than half a billion copies since the start of this publishing company in the 1970s. The most popular tract, *This Was Your Life!*, is said to have sold over eighty million copies, quite possibly making it the bestselling comic book of all time.

The tracts are produced to be cheap, printed in a small format with a black and white interior and a two-color cover, with a catchy title and an eye-catching cartoony image. They are meant to be given away, left in phone booths, etc.

Jack T. Chick is a cartoonist and has drawn many of the hundreds of tracts produced over the years himself. He has been assisted by the cartoonist Fred Carter, who never signs any of his work, but whose elaborate, realistic style is easily distinguishable from Chick's more cartoony drawings.

The stories in these tracts follow a few basic themes, almost all of them intent on convincing readers to fall to their knees and instantly confess their faith in Jesus Christ. Many tell stories of people dying and going to hell for not having accepted Jesus as their savior. Often Chick goes out of his way to make sure the reader understands that it doesn't matter how good, caring, and understanding they have been, they will still be eternally punished for their non-belief. To press the point home, these good people are often contrasted with real scumbags who live egotistical lives of murder and mayhem, but still go to heaven for having repented at the last moment.

Another theme is the bashing of other religions, such as Islam, but particularly Catholicism, for which Jack T. Chick has a special dislike. His

theories on the Catholic Church are a jumble of conspiracy theories sometimes so absurd that even the most ardent follower would be a bit skeptical.

The makers of the Chick Tracts are well aware of the potential of comics to reach an audience, as can be seen in this statement from their catalog: "The intriguing front cover, cartoon art, and dramatic stories make Chick Tracts irresistible." The deliberate use of images as a tool for communication is also evident in the way that the tracts have not only been translated into more than one hundred languages, but that there is a series of "black" tracts, where the characters have been redrawn so that black readers will identify with them more.

As an atheist, I am flabbergasted by the unreasonable tone, the literal interpretations of the Bible, and not least the blind zeal to convert people that permeate these frightening little publications. The Chick Tracts have been banned in Canada, labeled "hate literature," and I have to agree. There is sadly no love involved in the message of these fear-provoking, damning comics.

As in all Chick's publications, the readers are threatened with life in hell if they die without Jesus in their heart. This age-old threat becomes so much more scary when presented in a publication so obviously geared towards impressionable young kids. In the catalog for Chick Publications, you can read the following statement: "A little girl of 5 accepted the Lord as her savior when she and her mother read BEST FRIENDS." And in another part of the catalog, dedicated to spreading the word to children, it says: "It is estimated that 85% of those who become Christians do so between the ages of 4 and 18."

Religious Rants:
The Antichrist Revealed!

► One of the covers of the Alberto series, showing how—according to the comic—the Pope and the Cardinals of the Roman Catholic Church have supported the Nazis and the Communists, and how they were the masterminds behind the persecution of the Jews.

►► The Pope leading the four horsemen of the Apocalypse, from the cover of the fifth issue of the Alberto series, part of the ongoing *Crusaders* series.

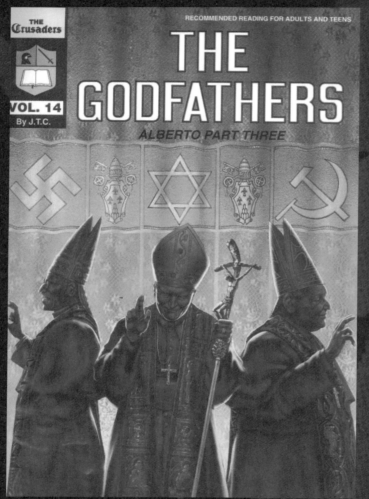

► According to Jack Chick, the Catholic system was behind the rise of the Nazi party, and is shown to have orchestrated the Holocaust.

The stage was being set for Germany's new Roman Catholic star. His name... **ADOLPH HITLER.**

A priest was busy writing a book for Hitler called **"MEIN KAMPF."**

The writer was the Jesuit father, Staempfle.[4]

This book was the master plan of the Jesuits for Hitler's take-over of Germany.

The Chick Tracts are not the only publications of Jack T. Chick. In another series of comic books, he also tells a story that is said to be based on the testimony of a supposedly ex-Jesuit priest, Alberto Rivera. There were six issues of this comic published between 1979 and 1988. They are still kept in print and can be ordered directly from Chick Publications.

Alberto narrates the comics, and as a frame story we follow his life. He was left by a devout Catholic mother to be a student at a religious school in Spain at the age of seven, and even though he harbored doubts he slowly rose in the ranks of the Catholic system. At the age of twenty-five he left the Catholic system to become one of its most prominent detractors. This framing story is only used, though, for the specific purpose of telling the "true" story behind the Roman Catholic Church, as seen through the eyes of a representative of the rival protestant movement.

These books set out to prove to the reader that the Roman Catholic Church is the work of the Devil, and that the Pope is the Antichrist mentioned in the Bible. The inferences made are horrendous, but always presented as "the truth." The Catholic system is presented as the result of the Roman emperors' wishes to retain control of "their" world. Among other things, Catholicism is "revealed" to be responsible for the start of both world wars; to be the instigator behind Islam as well as Communism; to have spies in high office all over the world; to have been behind the assassinations of both Lincoln and Kennedy; and so on. In essence, Catholicism is shown to cause all the evils of this world, and the next.

The makers of these comics have understood the basic premises of propaganda, and have made sure that the readers will be left in no doubt whatsoever. Much hinges on the belief in the existence of Alberto, and so each comic book starts with a page of photos of him, his I.D. card, and signed statements to the truth of his words by other ex-Catholics, among other things.

The series also sports the widely used tag "based on a true story," a statement which is slightly

AND THE BIBLE SAYS:

And there was weeping until the Lamb of God came forth to open the book.

It was, of course, the Lord Jesus Christ Himself.

The chapter goes on to describe the unspeakable joy and blessing in heaven through this act.

In chapter 6 of Revelation, Christ opens the first seal and reveals His arch enemy . . .

IT IS THE ANTICHRIST!*

"The papacy is the seat of the true and real Antichrist" . . . Martin Luther.

marred by the following text, found at the bottom of the first page: "No similarity between any names, characters, persons and/or institutions in this magazine with those of any living or dead person or institution is intended, and any such similarity which may exist is purely coincidental . . ."

Another way the makers of these comic books try to ensure that they are believed is the frequent use of quotations to prove that the things stated are based on facts. The only problem is that they mostly quote from other Jack T. Chick publications.

All in all, this is a brilliant piece of conspiracy theory, presented in comics form to sell its ideas to the masses, and thus makes fascinating reading.

Despite research by several major protestant newspapers, such as *Christianity Today, Cornerstone,* and *Forward*, which state that the story presented by Alberto is a fraud, Jack T. Chick Publications keeps these comics in print, and still promotes them as showing the truth. As shown on the previous pages, attacks on Catholicism can also be found in many of the tracts published by Jack T. Chick.

▲ **The Pope is "revealed" to be the Antichrist, as predicted in the book of Revelation in the Bible (well, according to Jack T. Chick anyway). . .**

The Catholics Strike Back!

▲ The American comics biography of John Paul II. Notice that this issue was approved by the Comics Code Authority—no profanity to be found here!

It is quite obvious that Jack T. Chick holds a grudge against Catholicism in general and the Pope in particular. There are several pages on the internet where Catholics respond to these criticisms, but there is no one refuting his claims via an equally megalomaniac propaganda campaign through comics. Comics seem sometimes to be deemed too frivolous a media to be used in the name of the Catholic God. That is not to say that there aren't any Catholic comics out there. To find proof of this, you need only visit *Festival International de la Bande Dessinée Angoulême*, the largest comics festival in Europe, and go into one of many large churches in the small French town of Angoulême. There you will inevitably find not only exhibitions about Catholic/Christian comics, but also a big market selling graphic novels with openly Catholic/ Christian themes.

Looking through all the examples I have found, there is one "hero" who seems to be the favorite of many of the cartoonists working with Catholic themes. It's the one, the only: Pope John Paul II! This is not especially surprising. Not only did Karol Józef Wojtyla (his name before he became the Pope) live an interesting and inspiring life, he was also the most respected and popular representative of the Catholic Church in the twentieth century.

In the French series of graphic novels called *Les chercheurs de Dieu* (*The Seekers of God*), the life of John Paul II is depicted in volume five from 1997, with other notables like Mother Theresa, Jesus, Jeanne d'Arc, and of course the Virgin Mary featuring in some of the other volumes. This is a biography trying to be as realistic as possible, both in the drawings and in the way the story is told, and it succeeds rather well, even if the result is slightly bland.

A more absorbing take on the same material can be found in the graphic novel *The Life of Pope John Paul II in Comics* by the Italians Alessandro Mainardi and Werner Maresta. This book has the added bonus of an introduction by "His Eminence Cardinal Jose Saraiva Martins, Prefect of the Congregation for Saints' Causes," as it says on the cover. Not a bad endorsement for a Catholic comic book. It resembles *The Seekers of God* in as much as the cartoonists are very devout in their treatment of the life of this holy man, but this comic has a much more engaging visual presentation, with beautiful, fully painted images.

An especially notable example is the comic book *The Life of Pope John Paul II*, published by Marvel Comics as early as 1982. This biography was written by Steve Grant and drawn by John Tartaglione and Joe Sinnott—all mostly known for making action and superhero comics. This comic came to be when a representative for Marvel gave a copy of Marvel's biography of St. Francis, *Francis, Brother of the Universe*, to the Pope's entourage, which resulted in the Pope agreeing to the production and assigning a lifelong friend, Father Mieczyslaw Malinski, to take part, revealing many facts about the Pope's life that had not been recorded before. During the production of this comic book, the Pope was shot, an event that was incorporated into the story. The result is the most engaging of all the biographies of the Pope that I have read, probably due to the years of experience all the professionals working on this project had from doing commercial comics.

There are other examples, such as the graphic novel *Pope John Paul II* by the Italian Toni Pagot, which contains yet another "straight" biography in comic form. And then there's the strangest of them all, *The Incredible Popeman*, a Colombian comic book by Rodolfo León Sánchez. This is stated to be a tribute to Pope John Paul II, reincarnating him as a superhero who uses superpowers to battle Satan and the forces of darkness. In this comic he is depicted with anti-demon gloves, an anti-sin shield, chastity underwear(!), rubber boots as a shield from divine electricity, a staff of light and faith, a holy Bible, holy water, and holy wine.

▼ OK, so *Battle Pope* is a satire and not a propaganda tool for the Catholic Church, but I just had to include it here. It's the story of a badass superhero-type character, who battles the Devil, hangs out with Jesus (called "J."), and constantly argues with God. No, it's definitely not John Paul II . . .

▼ *The Life of Pope John Paul II in Comics* by the Italians Alessandro Mainardi and Werner Maresta. A beautiful, modern version of the life of the world's most popular Pope.

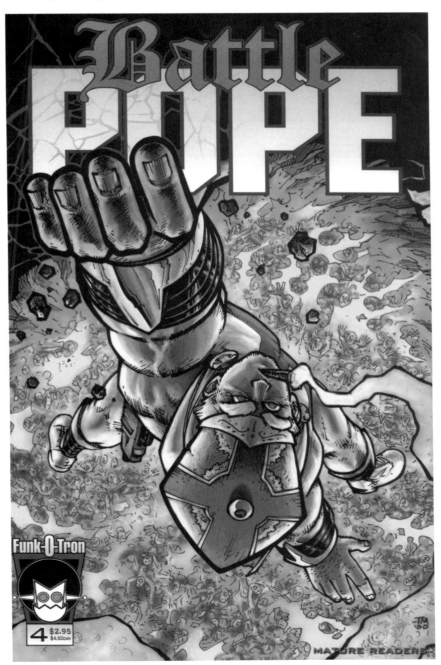

◄ In *The Life of Pope John Paul II*, the American writer uses several storytelling techniques that enhance the feeling of the story. Here we see the personal pronoun "me" used by a journalist writing about the Pope's life—giving the reader a possibility to see everything through his eyes—who observes the effect that the Pope's speech has on a group of young delinquents at Yankee Stadium.

Hansi: The Girl Who Loved the Swastika

▲ The cover to *Hansi: The Girl Who Loves the Swastika* must be one of the most striking covers ever made for a comic book. Al Hartley really outdid himself here, making sure that everyone would pick up a copy.

▶ Hansi getting excited because the Nazis bring books that make her mother's old Bible seem antiquated.

◄◄ **Hansi is very quickly swept away by the rhetoric of the Nazi party.**

◄ **Hansi finds her new religion: belief in the U.S.**

◄ **Another example of the Christian comics that Al Hartley made, here published by Barbour Christian Comics, who took over after Spire ceased publishing in the early 1980s. The story is based on the auto-biographical novel with the same title, written by David Wilkerson.**

One of the most successful series of religious comics of all time is the American Spire Christian Comics, and this mostly due to the professional cartoonist Al Hartley's conversion to Christ. In 1967 Hartley went to a prayer meeting and, moved by the sermon, "turned his life over to God—lock, stock, and drawing board." Within ten years he had converted twenty-six family members and dropped the secular comics he had been producing to focus on doing evangelical work through his comics.

At first he tried to inject Christian thought into the Archie comics he was working on, but was told by the publisher to tone down that aspect. Then came the opening he had hoped for, when the publisher Fleming H. Revell asked him to make comic books with stated Christian content. The series—with titles like *There's a New World Coming*, *The Cross and the Switchblade*, and *God's Smuggler*—was very successful and Hartley made about sixty Christian comics, including Bible story adaptations, biographical adaptations, and "Kiddies Christian Comics," all through the 1970s.

Of all these, one of the most memorable is *Hansi: The Girl Who Loved the Swastika* from 1973. This is the story of a young girl in Sudetenland, who, when the Germans invaded, was pleased because they brought books to read. Soon she wins an award for being a good student and is sent to Prague to become leader of the Hitler Youth. All through this, she is an undying believer in the Nazi party, saying things like, "We are nothing . . . The Reich is everything!" on being confronted with a disillusioned, blind soldier coming home from the front. When the war turns, she is put in a Russian labor camp, where all the women are raped at night except Hansi, who is deemed "too skinny." After escaping, she finally finds her way to an American camp, where to her surprise she is treated decently by the gum-chewing soldiers. After the war, she is reunited with her old boyfriend, but they are not happy together until he brings home a Bible and

they are rejuvenated by its message. Finally they move to America, where Hansi is astounded by the decadent lifestyles but sets out to love this country, which is, after all, "one nation under God," and runs Christian support groups in prisons and halfway houses all across California.

It's quite a fascinating tale and becomes even more so when you know that it was based on a true story. The *Hansi* comic book was part of a series of biographies of famous Christians in the 1970s, like the musician Johnny Cash, the football coach Tom Landry, and the concentration-camp survivor Corrie ten Boom. The *Hansi* comic book was based on the autobiography of Maria Anne Hirschmann, who actually lived through most of what is described in the comic.

OK, so it's based on a true story, but the treatment of the story is questionable. First, it's published by a Christian publishing company, so the moral should be quite obvious. Yet, here we meet a girl who at first only believes in the Bible, then suddenly only believes in *Mein Kampf*, and then goes back to only believing in the Bible. Not much of a statement for free thinking . . . And then there's the moral of the experience with the Russians, where Hansi is kept "pure" all the way through and is saved, but the other women who were raped were "rewarded" by being shot when they tried to escape.

The way Hansi is drawn throughout this comic is also problematic. Since she is supposed to be a pure and true "bride of Christ," she is not allowed to age noticeably in the comic, which is a problem when the story stretches on for decades. The real clincher is the last scene, when Hansi is giving a speech to the inmates of an American prison, retelling her life's experience and commenting that "None of you were born then"—while still looking exactly as she did during World War II.

Saved Through Archie Comics

Al Hartley did not rest on his laurels with the success of the Spire Christian Comics series. He was still producing Archie comics, but without too overtly Christian themes due to restrictions set out by the publisher.

But Hartley was determined to get his message across. He and his publisher at Spire Christian Comics, Fleming H. Revell, had an idea to do a separate series of Archie comics, specially designed to contain Christian messages. As Hartley himself described it, it was "a fantastic idea for evangelism," but there was just one hitch. The president of the company publishing the Archie comic books, John Goldwater (the same John Goldwater who was the key proponent of the comic book censorship guidelines known as the

Comics Code Authority), was Jewish. However, this did not stop him from giving Hartley and Revell permission to make these Christian comic books, and in 1973 the first Spire Christian Comics featuring Archie was published, called *Archie's One Way*.

All in all, nineteen of these Christian Archie comic books were produced during the 1970s and early 1980s, and they were kept in print for a long time, selling between ten and twenty million copies worldwide (the numbers vary somewhat, depending on the source). The series garnered quite a lot of interest from other media, and even led to Hartley writing an autobiography about his conversion to Christ, called *Come Meet My Friend*, which showed him on the cover surrounded by all the characters from Archie comics.

The stories in these Christian comic books looked just like ordinary Archie comics, since Hartley was one of the regular artists of the series all throughout the 1970s. The covers usually do not give them away as being anything but ordinary Archie comic books either, which was perhaps a conscious strategy to reach as wide an audience as possible. Many stories even start out as ordinary Archie stories, entertaining in their own right; but they soon reveal themselves as having a particular message to communicate.

Compared to the ruthlessly propagandistic comics of, say, the Chick Tracts, these comic books are pretty harmless, and quite a good read if you are prepared to forgive the rather cheesy moral often presented at the end of each chapter. In the stories, witnessing is a phenomenon often discussed—in other words the act of telling people of your own religious experience without attempting (too vigorously) to push it onto anyone—and I find these comics to work on that same, gentle level. Sure, they are sometimes preachy, but always on a very humane level. Due to the appeal of these characters, as well as the well-crafted art of Al Hartley and the very humane message, the Christian Archie comics were effective religious propaganda.

► One of many Christian Archie comic books, which were produced in the 1970s. They often used humor to "sell" Christian ideas. Here is a pun on the phenomenon of "witnessing," that is to tell people about your own religious beliefs and "show the way."

◄ A rather preachy episode of the Christian Archie comic book, using the Archie characters as mere propaganda puppets for the message to get through. The comment from Big Ethel at the end is really over the top.

Background illustration Here a poll at Riverdale High shows that the most popular teacher is . . . Jesus. I especially like Betty's assertion that Jesus' rise from the dead is ". . . one of the best recorded events in history!"

◄◄ *How to Become a Christian*—an easy four-step method presented in a Christian Archie comic book from the 1970s. The characters looking for salvation were never the Archie gang, who all seemed to be devout Christians, but characters probably designed to be like the average reader.

◄ All smiles, and no problems, at the local Bible Club. The reporter trying to find dissident views at Riverdale High has his job cut out for him. Everyone acts as if they have been drugged or hypnotized to only state the official truth "that everything is good." Even so, having white and black students hanging out together was still quite a statement in the early 1970s.

The Gospel According to Charles M. Schulz

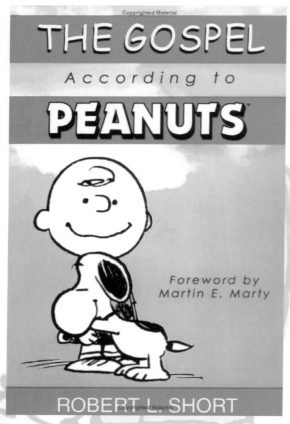

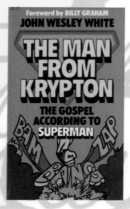

◀ *The Gospel According to Peanuts* and *The Parables of Peanuts* were two very influential books published in the 1960s, and are still kept in print. These books have been translated into many languages, as can be seen with the cover to the original book, published in Swedish in the 1960s.

◀ A lot of books have been written about religious subjects, using the popularity of comics to get their message across.

Peanuts by Charles M. Schulz was for a long time the most popular comic strip in the world. Running in thousands of newspapers, collected in best-selling trade paperbacks, spawning numerous animated TV shows, merchandise, etc., it was a seemingly all pervasive, ever-present phenomenon in the lives of fans all around the world. That this interest has barely waned can be seen in the success of the latest chronological and complete collections of the *Peanuts* strips, which are perennial bestsellers.

One notion about *Peanuts*, which has been discussed over and over again, is how much of a philosophical, religious, and even outright Christian message there is in the strip. The main proponent of these thoughts was Robert L. Short, who wrote two books on the matter: *The Gospel According to Peanuts* (1965) and *The Parables of Peanuts* (1968). These books have been reprinted numerous times, and are still in print today. The first book alone has sold more than ten million copies, a figure that has "no doubt topped the number of sales of all books in theology-not-associated-with-cartoons published since 1965," as Martin Marty writes in the foreword to an edition from the year 2000.

Short argues that *Peanuts* was a kind of witnessing on behalf of Schulz and that many of the virtues described in the Bible can be found in the cast of characters that Schulz created. Short's arguments are often convincing, especially since they are accompanied by numerous *Peanuts* strips that seem to convey the very message Short is looking for. On the other hand, he also tries to sell some rather fundamentalist ideas about who goes to heaven and what constitutes hell, which don't seem to be in keeping with the content of Schulz's comics at all.

These works by Short spawned a whole genre of books looking at perceived religious aspects of comics, like the rather unexpected *The Gospel According to Andy Capp* (by D. P. McGeachy III); the two equivalent *The Gospel According to Superman* (by John T. Galloway, Jr.) and *The Man from Krypton: The Gospel According to Superman* (by John Wesley White); and the most improbable of them all, *Good News for Grimy Gulch* (by the Methodist preacher Del Carter), which is about the obscure comic strip *Tumbleweeds*. There is even yet another book about *Peanuts*: *What's It All About, Charlie Brown?* (by Jeffrey H. Loria). These books are sometimes

▼ In this strip, Linus—the most fervent student of the Bible in *Peanuts*—reassures Lucy that the current rain will not instigate another biblical flood by quoting the ninth chapter of Genesis.

insightful, often preachy, and almost always trying just a bit too hard to prove their points.

As to the question of whether there is a message to be found in *Peanuts*. . . Well, that the characters in the comics discuss philosophical issues is quite evident when reading just a handful of strips. It is also evident that there are many references to Christian ideas, beliefs, and phenomena, such as the Bible and Bible School. There is also the fact that Charles M. Schulz was a Christian and never hid his personal religious commitment. He was a member of and a Sunday School teacher in the Church of God, a conservative Protestant denomination in the Pietist and Wesleyan tradition. But to extrapolate from all this that *Peanuts* is a Christian strip and that Schulz was witnessing to his readers is taking it too far, I think.

After reading books and articles about *Peanuts*, interviews with Schulz, and of course the actual *Peanuts* strips, I am convinced that many of the ideas put forth by Robert L. Short and other writers on this topic are erroneous, and say more about the authors and their ideas than about *Peanuts*. That said, I am also convinced that *Peanuts* does contain and transmit quite a lot of Christian ideas, and that it does so much more efficiently and effectively than any of the more didactic, propagandistic Christian comics discussed earlier in this chapter.

Treasure Chest of Fun and Fact?

Treasure Chest of Fun and Fact . . . There's something about a product where the makers have seen fit to include a positive description already in the name, like Quality Hotels, or Lucky cigarettes. I get suspicious from the get go and expect this euphemism to conceal a content that is actually not so good/worthwhile/delicious or whatever it is the title is trying to sell you. But when it comes to *Treasure Chest*, having read several decades' worth, I am not so sure this knee-jerk reaction is called for. For the readers at the time, this descriptive title was very likely true.

Let's get the basics down first. I have written about this comic book before in the chapter about Communism, but I felt it deserved an entry here as well. *Treasure Chest of Fun and Fact* was an American Catholic comic book, published first bimonthly and then monthly between 1946 and 1972. The publisher, George A. Pflaum, was a respected man, who was already publishing magazines like *Junior Catholic Messenger*, *Our Little Messenger*, and *Young Catholic Messenger*. These were all distributed directly as students' subscriptions at parochial schools; this was also the method used for *Treasure Chest*.

Treasure Chest contained stories that were, to a greater or lesser degree, about Catholic living and thinking, often focussing on what might be called "human values"—telling the stories of athletes, school children, and saints. According to The American Catholic History Research Center and University Archives (whew!), the intent of *Treasure Chest* was to "use the comics format to teach tenets of both Catholic faith and American patriotism." This may be, but the stories are not at all as preachy as many other didactic religious comics around. They are often educational and enlightening, but do not constantly come across as overt propaganda. This might have something to do with the contributors. The cartoonists working on *Treasure Chest* were no hacks. Many of them were—and still are—respected names associated with more mainstream publishers, names like Reed Crandall,

Graham Ingels, and Joe Orland from EC, Joe Sinnott from Marvel Comics, and Murphy Anderson and Jim Mooney from DC Comics. Perhaps this was because the publisher of *Treasure Chest* never demanded that the cartoonists working on the comics be Catholics themselves.

One intriguing question that this comic book raises is why the editor felt the need to join the Comics Code Authority (see Chapter Four for a discussion of the Code), and submit their comics in order to get the seal of approval on the cover. Considering that there were publishers who had decided not to use the Code (such as Dell Comics, publishing the unassailable Disney comics, and Gilberton, depending on the reputation of *Classics Illustrated* as a safe educational tool), they were in no way obliged to do so, not the least since they were almost never distributed through regular newsstands. Perhaps the printer demanded it, or maybe the publisher thought it was a way to contribute to a good cause. Either way, the content of *Treasure Chest* was more than likely already close to perfection in the eyes of the people at the Comics Code Authority.

Treasure Chest lasted more than five hundred issues, making it one of the longest running comic books in America and certainly the longest running containing non-fiction. I have not found any reliable sources to the print runs of this comic book, but to last that long it must have done a good job of reaching, informing, and imbueing "proper" Catholic values in young Catholics during its twenty-six-year existence.

▶ The covers of *Treasure Chest* tell their own story. Some were outright religious in theme, others political and/or historical, and some just comical. Notice the seal of approval from the Comics Code Authority.

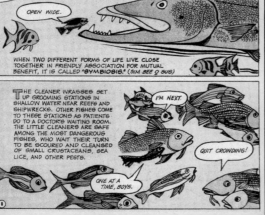

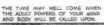

◄◄ Some o...
in *Treasure*...
about scienc...
The Story of...
where the a...
explain why...
complemen...
in nature—...
course ment...
or natural s...

◄ An open...
Catholic liv...
response to...
threats, fro...
of *Treasure*...
priest is Fat...
also had a c...
issue called...
with Father...
most propag...
part of the w...

Amar Chitra Katha: Classics Illustrated India

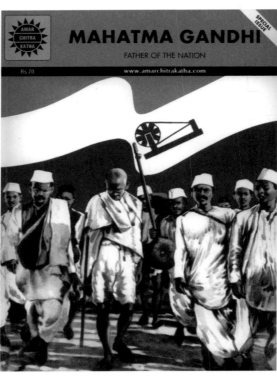

◄◄ In the comics series *Amar Chitra Katha*, you will find not only stories based on Indian and Hindu myths and fables, but also stories about other great spiritual leaders like Zarathustra, Jesus, and Buddha.

◄ *Amar Chitra Katha* presents the leaders that helped build modern-day India, and in doing so helped build a sense of unity among the people of India.

The comics market in India is huge, partly because India is a country with more than one billion citizens, and partly because the English language heritage has given access to the comics culture of the U.S. One influence from the U.S. that is especially evident is the didactic comic book series called *Classics Illustrated*, which consists of short versions of classical books, but also biographies of famous people.

In India, this inspired the creation of the comic book series *Amar Chitra Katha* (*Immortal Captivating Stories*) in 1967 by Anant Pai, who wanted to educate the people of India. He was dismayed to find that Indian students knew more about Greek and Roman mythology than about their own history and mythology. Anant Pai therefore set out to educate his people, through

comics, about their cultural heritage. And he did a very good job of it. Today, there are more than four hundred titles in the ever expanding line of *Amar Chitra Katha*; they have sold more than ninety million copies worldwide and have been translated into twenty different Indian languages, as well as into French, Spanish, and German. But most importantly, the *ACK* line of comic books have reached generation after generation of Indians and shaped their images of what India is and can be.

The critics of the *ACK* comics hold forth that many were produced in a hurry, without allowing time to check facts and make sure that background and clothing were accurate, and insist that they be viewed as fiction and not as fact. But this has not hindered parents and teachers in India from using them extensively as educational aids.

▶ The producers of *Amar Chitra Katha* have been accused of racism, of perpetuating the notion of separate castes in India by portraying representatives of the lowest caste, the "untouchables," with darker skin, curly hair, and bigger noses.

▶▶ The style used in many of the comics in the *Amar Chitra Katha* series looks surprisingly similar to the style often used in *Classics Illustrated*, with the exception that many heroes/gods are blue. . .

The homogenized and unbiased ways in which these comics describe Indian culture (as with *Classics Illustrated*, the creators seem to have been under strict orders to tone down controversies and violence) have probably been part of the process of promoting national integration.

Reading the *ACK* comic books, it is evident how much they have been inspired by *Classics Illustrated*. Not only do they use similarly realistic, fifties-style artwork, the same page-layouts (with much of the information given in captions), and the same color scheme (with few bright colors), they also share the same didactic purpose. Comparing the two, I find the *ACK* comics a slightly better read, as they seem to have a better flow when telling a story.

The *ACK* comics are still sold today all over India and are so pervasive that for many they have defined the way Indian gods and goddesses look, how various historical events really took place, and which stories make up the collected canon of Indian myths and fables. It has been said that the *ACK* comics filled the void left by storytelling grandmothers and grandfathers as India moved from the traditional system of extended families to a more urban way of living. The choice of English as the major language also made sure that the comic reached children and young adults studying English at school. All in all, *Amar Chitra Katha* is one of the most effective pieces of propaganda ever produced using comics as the medium.

Hairy Polarity:
The Dangers of Harry Potter

$2.95 USA $4.95 CAN

▲ The comic book
*Hairy Polarity and the
Sinister Sorcery Satire*
is an attack on the Harry
Potter phenomenon
from a fundamentalist
Christian viewpoint.

◄◄ **Here we see little Sebastian, who has been brave and told his friends that he thinks he is gay, getting set "on the right track." There is another comic about the dangers of homosexuality from Revival Fires, drawn in a more classical realistic way, with an adult protagonist. Reading it makes me realize just how vile I think this version is, using the now popular manga style to reach out to kids.**

◄ **The nauseatingly preachy ending to** *Hairy Polarity***, where all is well, everyone loves each other, and the ever-doubting Minnie finally sees the right way and embraces Jesus as her savior.**

◄◄ **To prove just how despicable Harry Potter really is, it is revealed in** *Hairy Polarity* **that the author, here called Verbosi, has just been channeling the words from a demon.**

◄ *The Truth for Youth* **is a new version of the New Testament with added comics sections, presenting the readers with "absolute truths" about such interesting topics as safe sex, abortion, and rock music!**

Harry Potter is without a doubt the biggest phenomonon to hit the youth of the world in the last decade, with the books outselling almost everything else. The author, J. K. Rowling, has received praise for inspiring a whole new generation—previously mostly into movies and computer games—to take a renewed interest in reading.

Not everybody has been happy with this state of affairs, however. The self-proclaimed evangelist Tim Todd, who runs the publisher Revival Fires International, is quite sure about the bad influence Harry Potter has on the youth of today: "The Harry Potter books present a Godless universe, one in which the most powerful wizards win. In these books the hero is a wizard who shows no evidence of belief in God and does not use the power of prayer to combat evil. This is not the vision of the universe that Christian parents wish to instill in their children, nor is 'white' magic an appropriate response to evil."

To combat this bad influence Todd has published the comic book *Hairy Polarity and the Sinister Sorcery Satire*. Again, according to Todd: "The *Hairy Polarity* comic book creatively informs the reader of the many explicit examples of appalling evil in the Harry Potter Movie, such as blood sacrifice, animal sacrifice, demon possession, levitation, divination, shifting humans into animals, communing with the dead, bringing evil wizards back from the dead through the shedding of blood, only to mention a few."

Hairy Polarity is drawn and written by the pseudonymous Jonako, with co-scripter Nate Butler and inker Carlos Garzón. They have all done a reasonable job of it and present a good satire on *Harry Potter* up until the end, where

the over-pedagogical Christian message gets too much in the way. All the same, I can't help but wonder how successful this comic book is in informing the reader of the sinful quality of all things magical, when they are presented in a rather cool and visually interesting way. And does the evangelist actually mean that he believes in white magic?

The *Hairy Polarity* comic is also included in a comic adaptation of the New Testament called *The Truth for Youth*, which has, according to the publisher, 1.2 million copies distributed ". . . in an attempt to respond to the liberal agenda that is being promoted aggressively in public schools." *Hairy Polarity* is only one of many comics in *The Truth for Youth*. On their website one can read that the comics "tell the youth the absolute truth about the moral issues confronting them today." These "absolute truths" are presented as such hot topics as Pornography, Homosexuality, Safe Sex, Abortion, Rock Music, School Violence, Evolution, Drugs, Drunkenness, and Peer Pressure.

Now these comics are all well drawn and quite well written too, but like the one about *Harry Potter*, they get rather annoying when the dogmatic message is delivered and they all turn preachy. I have a hard time seeing a young reader of the twenty-first century buying into any of the things presented here, like the suggestion that homosexuality is a sin or that evolution is a lie. But I may be wrong.

A panel from *Bringing up Father* by George McManus. Beautiful maidens are used to contrast with the wife of the main character, Jiggs, who is discouraged from joining the fun at the beach when he hears that his wife also wants to get into a bathing suit.

Chapter 6
Sexual Slander

◄ *Bizarre Sex* was an American magazine with just that: stories about "bizarre" sex. The cover of this issue from 1984 was made by Richard Corben.

◄ A woodcut print, issued in the UK in 1913, and colored by hand. Produced by the Suffrage Atelier, a society formed in 1909 to "encourage artists to forward the Woman's Movement, and particularly the enfranchisement of women, by means of pictorial publications."

▲ Alison Bechdel, creator of the biweekly *Dykes to Watch Out For* and the prize-winning graphic novel *Fun Home*, often has a message in her comics, even though they are also meant to entertain. This strip was specially commissioned for the book *Transgender Warrior* by Leslie Feinberg, though, and was quite obviously made with the express purpose of sending a message.

Sex and Comics!

I knew I'd get your attention with that title. There are a number of reasons why sex and comics are two things that, when put together, make people react.

The first and probably most common is the widespread misconception that comics are for kids and kids only. Someone armed with this notion and also harboring preconceived ideas about what is and what is not suitable for a child to read might very well react to "unsuitable" content in comics, no matter if the comics in question were initially intended for children or not. This has happened over and over again, all throughout the last century. And sadly it still happens today, since this notion seems to be extremely long-lived.

Considering that sexuality is a very sensitive topic, not the least in association with children, this has led to a lot of self-censoring in comics, making many of them antiseptically free of all references to sex, including (the indicative) parent-child relationships—such as in the Disney comics,

where relationships tend to be uncles/aunts and nephews/nieces.

This notion also varies from country to country. When manga hit the West, many readers were flabbergasted by the often quite sexual portrayals of young girls in comics made for young girls. These depictions did not at all correspond to the way girls were portrayed in the (few) comics produced in the West for young female readers.

Another problem, maybe not so damning for comics as the first one but still a factor to take into account, is that comics is a visual medium and thus habitually judged differently than "mere" texts (which in comparison are deemed less directly subversive). Images are powerful in the way they influence how we view the world. Many people are very well aware of this and are either making use of this knowledge or making a big fuss over the ones who do. Add sexuality into this mix, and the debates can get very heated indeed.

When it comes to sex, there are also lots of different ideas about what is acceptable in popular culture and art. Some think that the merest indication of sexuality is too much, whereas for others, anything goes. Add to this the fundamental fact that we all have different ideas about what sexuality is (and/or gender for that matter), and what is and what isn't "normal," and the confusion is complete.

Comics are a part of the society in which they were created, and this shows in the diverse ways in which gender and sex are dealt with within this art form. But does this mean that there is propaganda in comics using themes of gender and human sexuality? Oh, certainly! As I have stated before, there are always two sides to every argument and you can find—as I will show in this chapter—examples of everything from comics used, more or less subliminally, to reproduce the "normal" hetero-sexual, male-dominated world order, to comics seeking to punctuate this very idea and show the "perverted" alternatives available.

▶ **Prism Comics is a** "nonprofit organization, promoting the work of lesbian, gay, bisexual, and transgender creators in comics, as well as LGBT issues in comics," according to the colophon in their yearly publication with the same name.

Background illustration
In the book *Einsteins fru* (*The Wife of Einstein*) from 2008, Swedish artist Liv Strömqvist discusses the way various famous men have treated their wives. In the case of Einstein, Strömqvist shows how his wife contributed early onto most of Albert's discoveries, but later on had her status diminished to housewife and caretaker of their children, until Albert finally left her for a younger woman.

Harlots and Hags

Reading comics from many parts of the world, especially older comics, it soon becomes evident that there is a tendency to frequently depict "the other"—as discussed in the earlier chapter on racism in comics. What this "other" is varies across the globe, but there is one "other" that seems to be constant in most countries: the female.

This is because cartoonists in these countries have predominantly been male, and have told and drawn stories from their perspective. Add to this the tendency of cartoonists to simplify in order to communicate and you get an oversimplified version of the fairer sex—not in all comics, but in quite a lot of them.

This has resulted in there being only a few variations of women in comics. In short, they can be generalized into the three "classic" categories of the virgin, the mother, and the crone. Think about the opening scene in Shakespeare's *Macbeth*, with the three witches ("When shall we three meet again . . ."), and you get the picture. In literature and in theories on female representation in popular culture, these types have been expanded to include several other recurring ways in which female characters are depicted, but in comics, I would say that female depictions in a large section of the medium can actually be boiled down to just two: the maiden/vamp and the mother/old hag.

The maiden/vamp is an often extremely sexually exaggerated female character that is used as an object of desire, as someone to rescue, or as merely the beautiful token to be at the side of the male main character. The mother/hag is the extreme opposite, usually depicted as dominating a well-domesticated husband, drawn as unsexy, and often downright ugly. These are all over comics, from humor comics to adventure comics, and all over the world. For a perfect example of both, look at *Bringing up Father* by George McManus, an American comic strip from the first half of the twentieth century. The main character's wife is a dominating, often seemingly ill-willed woman who beats her husband, while his daughter is a stereotypical good-looking and very nice young woman/girl.

An interesting variation on this was presented by the cartoonist Alison Bechdel (*Dykes to Watch Out For, Fun Home*), who identified at least four ways in which female characters were portrayed (derogatively) in comics:

Woman as a Mutant, that is, as something from another species altogether. This might sound strange, but look at a comic like *Garfield* and you will see that females are depicted as almost coming from another planet. Men are the norm, and women have to be depicted in a totally different form in order to separate them properly.

Woman as a Drag Queen, i.e. as a male with female "accessories." Think about the visual relationship between Mickey and Minnie Mouse or Donald and Daisy Duck and you get the picture. Start with a male character, add long eyelashes, a big, red mouth, and perhaps a skirt and a pink bow somewhere to top things off. Breasts are optional, at least in children's comics.

Woman as Fetish, i.e. the exaggeration of sexual features on female characters in comics where men are allowed to look "ordinary" and more anatomically correct. Bechdel herself refers to the classic comic strip *Blondie*, where the main character is very much sexually exaggerated, while her husband Dagwood looks like something the cat dragged in. This is present in so many comics that I can't even begin to list them all.

All-Male Revue, which is strangely pervasive, sometimes with a token girl/woman thrown in. The most obvious example is, of course, *The Smurfs* by the Belgian artist Peyo; they were a group of little blue creatures, all living in a village together. Each had his separate individual character, such as the strong one, the one who can cook, or the one who is good at football—and then there was one who was a girl . . .

▼ *The Smurfs* by the Belgian Peyo is a perfect example of the all-male cast of many comics. Often it is not as evident as this, but compare this with, for instance, classics like *Tintin* or *Spirou and Fantasio* from Europe, or *Dick Tracy* and *Beetle* *Bailey* from the U.S., and it becomes apparent that it is an all-boys club.

▲▲ In *Bringing up Father* by George McManus, beautiful maidens/vamps were often contrasted with the main character's wife, who was often seen wielding household appliances, planning to hit him over the head. Here Jiggs is discouraged from joining the fun at the beach when he hears that his wife also wants to get into a bathing suit.

▲ The female characters in Disney comics are really a kind of Drag Queen, as Alison Bechdel puts it, as the differences with the male characters are all in the props they wear. Here is an early example of *Mickey Mouse* from 1931 by Floyd Gottfredson, and in the background on the facing page, *Donald Duck* from 1953 by the old master Carl Barks.

▲ The alien-looking Dagwood and his wife, the very sexy Blondie— now how did that attraction happen? Art by Chic Young from 1968.

▲ In *Fantastic Four*, created by Stan Lee and Jack Kirby in 1961, the token woman of the team, Susan Storm, had the distinctive characteristics of being the girlfriend of the genius hero and the ability to become invisible. A very adequate metaphor for the role women are often given in comics.

Wimmin's Comix

◄ *Wimmen's Comix* was an early all-female, ongoing comics anthology, which broke a lot of new ground and gave female cartoonists a way of expressing themselves. From the collection of Trina Robbins.

Women have been portrayed in the way shown on the previous pages because most of the cartoonists in the West have been male. This is changing as more and more women are getting into comics, both as readers and creators, but it has been a slow process.

In America, the explicit and outspoken predecessor of this development was a group of cartoonists working in the underground movement in the 1970s. They were disgusted by the way their male counterparts were portraying women, and by the fact that female cartoonists were never published in the almost exclusively male-edited and published comics anthologies. Therefore they chose to start their own, separatist comic book called *Wimmen's Comix* in 1972.

There were forerunners, like the single issue *It Ain't Me Babe* from 1970 and the anthology *Tits and Clits*, published the same year as *Wimmen's Comix*. But *Wimmen's Comix* (later changed to *Wimmin's Comix*, so as to not include the word "men" in the title) was the longest lasting of these efforts to put forth the ideas of female cartoonists.

It started up as a collective endeavor and had a system of rotating editors and much input from the others in the group calling themselves Wimmen's Comix Collective. This group included Sharon Rudahl, Terry Richards, Lee Marrs, Trina Robbins, Pat Moodian, Aline Kominsky, Michelle Brand, Lora Fountain, Shelby Sampson, Karen Marie Haskell, and Janet Wolfe.

▼ This comic was made by Trina Robbins, who not only was one of the first feminist cartoonists in America, but has also become comics' only "herstorian," making some of the few books on women and comics in the world. From the collection of Trina Robbins.

▼ In the comic book *It Ain't Me Babe*, the cartoonists used famous comic characters to show how unequal and biased their roles and relationships were in the original, male-oriented comics. From the collection of Trina Robbins.

▼ *It Ain't Me Babe* was published in 1970, making it the earliest all-female comic book in America. From the collection of Trina Robbins.

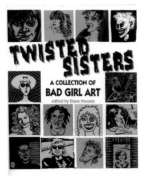

▲ *Twisted Sisters* was another all-female anthology, published in the 1990s. Some of the artists had been around since *Wimmen's Comix*, and some were new. The torch was passed on.

Wimmin's Comix lasted until 1991, when it was finally canceled, and during these years it helped a whole new generation of female American cartoonists get started, like Melinda Gebbie, Roberta Gregory, Penny Van Horn, M. K. Brown, Carol Tyler, Chris Powers, Carol Lay, and Mary Fleener. Many went on to make their own comic books, comic strips, and graphic novels, and little by little they changed the view of comics as an all-boys club.

The comics—or comix, as they were called at the time—in *Wimmin's Comix* were not always political, but quite often they were. They were not always about sex either, but again quite often so. Just making a separatist, feminist comic book was (and probably still is) a statement in itself, in that it gave female cartoonists a chance to express their views. Reading *Wimmin's Comix* and other later anthologies like *Twisted Sisters*, it becomes evident that not only did these female cartoonists have another outlook on life, but many of them also felt a need to be more or less openly feminist in what they talked about and how they portrayed the issues they wanted to raise, since their voices were much less heard, in comics and in society in general.

Just how efficient these comics were is hard to say. *Wimmin's Comix* and other all-female comic books were often neglected and discriminated against by society, but they did eventually give rise to a whole generation of female, and often politically aware, cartoonists in America, and their work has certainly made a difference.

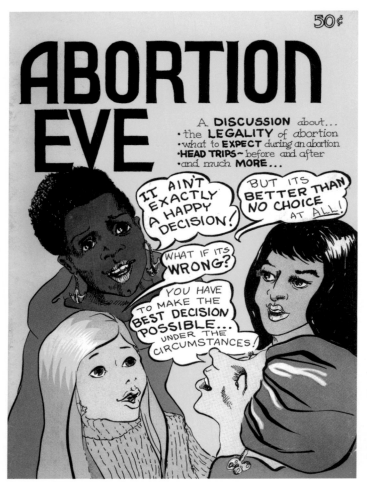

▲ *Abortion Eve* was a comic book from 1973 with a pro-choice message. It explains how an abortion works.

▶ The back cover of *Abortion Eve* shows a variation of the Holy Virgin Mary with the face of Alfred E. Neuman, the poster boy of *MAD Magazine*. Quite a provocative image.

▲ The Chick Tract *Who Murdered Clarice?* is an anti-abortion, pro-life publication by Jack T. Chick, from 2000. It tells the reader that abortion is a sin and that not only will the women who have abortions go to hell, but so will the politicians who uphold laws that make abortion possible.

Who Killed Abortion Eve?

◀ **Most of the arguments in *Abortion Eve* are fairly balanced, but sometimes the authors go a bit too far in trying to show the benefits of abortion, as in this scene where the older women almost only have bad things to say about having children when trying to persuade the younger woman to do away with her unwanted pregnancy.**

***Background illustration* In *Abortion Eve*, the cartoonists use five different women, all from different walks of life, in order to show different situations for women contemplating abortion.**

A subject that has provoked some of the most intense debates across many societies is abortion. In America this debate reached a fever pitch in 1973, when the case Roe v. Wade—in which the United States Supreme Court was to decide whether abortion was legal—captured the imagination of a whole nation. Opinions were divided, and all means were used to sway public opinion concerning the decision, including comic books, which were utilized by both sides.

A propaganda comic from this period that particularly stands out is the comic book *Abortion Eve*. It was published in 1973 by the small independent publisher Nannygoat Productions, who were in fact the two creators of the book, Joyce Farmer and Lyn Chevely, who had decided they wanted to do something about the male-dominated comics business. They were also both single mothers, and both working at a free women's clinic, who saw a need for a comic that explained abortion clearly.

Drawn by Farmer and written by Farmer and Chevely, the story features five women, all of whose names are variations of the biblical character Eve—Eva, Evelyn, Eve, Evita, and Evie—who meet at an abortion clinic and are treated by the counselor Mary Multipary. They each have different reasons for terminating their pregnancies, and Farmer and Chevely use these characters to create an interesting story while at the same time educating readers about abortion (which had just become legal due to the ruling in Roe v. Wade). The story is a bit ham-fisted, but it was very influential at the time.

There can be no doubt as to the intentions of Farmer and Chevely. The text on the insides of the cover bears the question, "Are some people more likely to suffer from 'unwanted pregnancy' than others?" It states that no Presidents of the United States, Generals of the Army, Admirals of the Navy, bank presidents, nuclear physicists, pipe fitters, or sanitary engineers have "contracted this malignant plague," but that typists, nurses, secretaries, welfare mothers, and sopranos are the ones who suffer from it the most. Times have moved on since this statement was made, but it is still a hard-hitting simile to show that this is an issue that concerns women but is decided by men.

The pro-life side argued at the time—and still argues—that all abortions are murder and should be treated as such. There were even comics made to promote this idea, such as *Who Killed Junior?*, also from 1973, the first and at the time largest anti-abortion handout ever, courtesy of the just two-month-old organization Right to Life. This was a small leaflet, depicting a newly conceived child as a cute cartoon character and very drastically showing how it is killed by the different abortions techniques. The leaflet ends with quotes from the Bible and comparisons between abortions and the actions of the Nazis during World War II. Not very subtle, then.

From our perspective, all of this was long, long ago in the early 1970s. So much has changed since then, but not the rhetoric of the religiously motivated pro-life group. In the tract *Who Murdered Clarice?*, published in the year 2000 and still in print, Jack T. Chick was obviously inspired by the leaflet *Who Killed Junior?*, presenting much the same case, only with far more fire and brimstone, essentially saying that all involved in an abortion will go to hell. Only the aborted babies will go to heaven, which is slightly strange as it implies that the ones performing and getting the abortions are doing a good, Christian thing . . .

Sex Education Funnies

The underground movement in American comics coincided with the hippie era, a time when "sex, drugs, and rock 'n' roll" was the abiding theme. This was mirrored in the comics, in which cartoonists took every opportunity to deal with subject matters that had hitherto been banned from the medium, not least by the Comics Code Authority. This new found freedom of visual expression included sex.

In an era of free love—that is, sex—one of the more unexpected underground comic books was *Incredible Facts o' Life: Sex Education Funnies* from 1972. This informational/educational comic book was published by the Multi-Media Resource Center and printed by Rip-Off Press, one of the major publishers of underground comics. *Incredible Facts o' Life* was an anthology, and the list of contributors reads like a who's who of the underground era: Terry Balawejder, Michele Brand, Robert Crumb, Shary Flenniken, Lora Fountain, Gary Frutkoff, Gary Halgreen, Bobby London, Ted Richards, Gilbert Shelton, and J. A. Smith.

What differentiates this from many other informational/educational comic books is that it was made by cartoonists who quite obviously had a lot to say about the subject and were not just hired to illustrate a script written by someone only out to convey a message. The stories all live up to the tag line "Sex Education *Funnies*" in that they are told with a zest and a humorous twist, which feels really fresh in comparison to many other comics I have read while researching this book.

The cartoonists in question also made use of some of the most famous characters in underground comics. The Fabulous Furry Freak Brothers all get "the clap" (gonorrhea) courtesy of Shelton, and Flenniken's Trots and Bonnie go to a free clinic to get a pelvic examination. Bobby London's *Sins of the Flesh!* portrays the problems of venereal disease in London's cutesy style, with the disease shown as the character Clarence Crablicé . . .

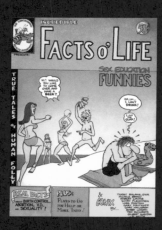

◄ *Incredible Facts o' Life: Sex Education Funnies* was an informational comic book about venereal disease, birth control, abortion, and sexuality published in 1972 in the middle of the underground movement in American comics.

Another effective story is *Preggers* by London and Robert Crumb, in which a woman (Strawberry Field—the Last of the Flower Kids) is pregnant, and her boyfriend (Buck Wheat Florida, Jr.) isn't very keen on having a baby. This story is told in Crumb and London's usual zany, action-packed, and humorous style, but discusses the issue of illegal versus legal abortion.

The center spread of the comic book contains *The Abortion Game* by Lora Fountain. This was a comment on the ongoing debate on the legalization of abortion (see the previous pages' Who Killed Abortion Eve?). It was made as a traditional board game, where only women were allowed to play (and men as partners with a woman). The game is shaped as the symbol of abortion and the steps include decisions that a pregnant woman has to make. Strikingly effective propaganda as it uses the positive associations of a game to convey a serious message.

All in all, I think *Incredible Facts o' Life: Sex Education Funnies* is a successful piece of propaganda. Information on its print run and distribution is hard to come by, but I think it is fairly certain that it spoke directly to the intended audience and that the ones it reached were likely to have been influenced by its messages.

◀◀ **A beautiful page from Bobby London's comic** *Sins of the Flesh!*, **featuring Clarence Crablicé, about how the main character gets gonorrhea, here portrayed as cute little bugs.**

◀ **In a collaboration with Bobby London, Robert Crumb tells the story of "Strawberry" Fields and "her old man" Buck Wheat Florida, Jr., in** *Preggers*. **The man has a predictable reaction to the news that Strawberry is pregnant and, as can be seen, the moral of the story is up for debate.**

◀◀ **Gilbert Shelton contributes with a story of how all the Fabulous Furry Freak Brothers get "the clap" from having sex with the same woman. Acting in character, they are not very responsible about it, but Shelton still manages to get a message across of the problems of venereal disease.**

◀ **Shary Flenniken uses her childlike characters Trots and Bonnie to talk about serious issues like birth control and sexually transmitted diseases in a very disarming way.**

◄◄ *AARGH!* was published in 1988 as a direct response to the controversial Section 28, an anti-gay amendment to the British Local Government Act. Cover by Bill Sienkiewicz.

◄ The story *The Mirror of Love* was recently remade as a graphic novel, where the images of Bissette and Veitch are replaced with photographs by José Villarrubia.

◄ Alan Moore's own contribution to *AARGH!*, *The Mirror of Love*, is an attempt to explain the history of homosexuality. As is often the case with Moore's comics, he uses an advanced combination of words and images, allowing for the different styles of Steve Bissette and Rick Veitch to play off each other.

◄◄ A page from the comic *From Homogenous to Honey* by Neil Gaiman, Bryan Talbot, and Mark Buckingham from *AARGH!* The character goes on to eradicate everything even remotely homosexual from the history of mankind, ending up with faceless people, all exactly the same. A powerful allegory, using the mask as a symbol of the face of the people behind Section 28.

► The final sequence from Art Spiegelman's contribution to *AARGH!*, entitled *Real Dream*. As can be seen, this comic was from 1974, but was reprinted as it conveyed a sentiment that fit this publication exactly.

AARGH!

Sex in comics has proven to be a difficult theme, and sex between two people of the same . . . well . . . sex, even more so. Homosexuality has been, and sadly still is, a hot topic, within and outside the world of comics. Still, if you look at this and many other phenomena in society, at least there seems to be a steady progression towards a greater tolerance and understanding. This might be an illusion, though, as setbacks do occur.

One such setback was the so-called Section 28, an anti-gay amendment to the British Local Government Act in the late 1980s. This was at a time when AIDS was heavily debated, and many pointed their fingers at the gay community as the culprits of this seemingly unstoppable plague. The response from the British government was to try to ban even the mentioning of homosexuality, reasoning that this would make it go away altogether. The amendment stated that a local authority "shall not intentionally promote homosexuality or publish material with the intention of promoting homosexuality," or "promote the teaching in any maintained school of the acceptability of homosexuality as a pretended family relationship." Considering that this was Great Britain and the year 1986 (and not Oceania and 1984 . . .), it is mind-boggling that the law was actually passed.

The comics anthology *AARGH!* (Artists Against Rampant Government Homophobia) was one of many reactions to this strange piece of legislation.

The book was published by Alan Moore at his newly started company Mad Love Publishing in 1988, in direct answer to Section 28, donating all the revenues to The Organisation for Lesbian and Gay Action, which was also formed in response to Section 28.

AARGH! is a fascinating book, to say the least, containing comics by a star-studded list of creators, including Brian Bolland, Neil Gaiman, Dave Gibbons, Harvey Pekar, Bill Sienkiewicz, Dave Sim, Posy Simmonds, Art Spiegelman, and Frank Miller. As with all anthologies, some contributions are more interesting than others.

One striking piece is Brian Bolland's single page, simply depicting Bolland as he sits at his drawing table talking about Section 28, condemning censorship but at the same time admitting homophobic tendencies within himself.

The most poignant contribution comes from Moore himself, *The Mirror of Love*, illustrated by Steve Bissette and Rick Veitch. In this mere eight-page story, Moore attempts to delineate the whole history of homosexuality, and to do so in a poem. A seemingly impossible task, which he pulls off beautifully.

AARGH! is long out of print, but there is a beautiful remake of Moore, Bissette, and Veitch's contribution by the colorist and photographer José Villarrubia, published as a book in its own right, with texts about Section 28. Villarrubia has a long relationship with *The Mirror of Love*, having also adapted it into a stage performance.

AARGH! was published in 1988 and a lot has happened in the years since, in comics and in the wider world. Section 28 has been repealed and homosexuality is more accepted, but in Moore's words from 1988: "As we approach the future, will Utopia's spires hove into view, or Death-camp Chimney stacks? My love, I wish I knew."

Voices from the Field

Not only can comics be a very potent tool for propaganda, but also an inexpensive and easily accessible one. This is something that the organization World Comics has taken to heart. The organization was started in Finland by Leif Packalén and has now spread to various parts of the globe, not least to India, where its sister organization, World Comics India, has been active for some time.

World Comics promotes the use of local comics as a means for social change, mostly through what they call "grassroots comics." This is a simple and ingenious way of using the cheapest means possible to create comics, while still getting the maximum effect. Representatives from World Comics travel around, teaching people in the remotest villages how to make comics using a few set rules. One is to only use one sheet of standard-sized paper, which is commonly available everywhere and fits into any copying machine. Another is to use only black and white, so as to make the comics cheap to reproduce. They also provide a model for the page with four identical panels and room for a title at the top. All of this helps people who are going to be making comics for the first time, as it sets out clear and simple rules that make the process manageable.

When reading the comics that have come out of the workshops of World Comics India over the last couple of years, what strikes you is the power of these simple and often crudely drawn comics. This is one of the basic ideas of grassroots comics, that they should be produced locally so that they use the right kinds of clothing, dialects, and so on to speak directly to the intended audience, instead of being produced somewhere far away by

◄◄ An explanation of how to make grassroots comics by Sharad Sharma, who is the president of World Comics India. Here you see the simple and effective method of grassroots comics, which is being taught by the representatives of World Comics.

◄ Here is a story of a girl in a village who wants to study to become a doctor, but is not allowed to by her parents. A few days later her brother falls ill and dies due to the fact that there was no doctor nearby. The parents then see the error of their ways and accept that girls should be allowed to study. Story and art by Swati Singh.

professional cartoonists with only a rudimentary feel for these facts.

Another striking thing is that many of the participants are female. We are seeing a change in this area in the West, but comics are still pretty much perceived as being produced for male readers here. In India this preconceived notion does not seem to be present and many of the participants in these workshops have been women. Obviously this means that the topics are presented from a female point of view, which is very enlightening. There are still a lot of problems in India when it comes to female liberation and equality, and this is often addressed in the grassroots comics.

Reading through, you get a picture of life as a woman in India. There are stories about the ancient

and degrading system of dowry, that is, the amount of money that the parents of a girl are supposed to pay to get her married (a major contributing factor to female infants being killed); self-empowerment through self-employment and organization among women; witch-hunting; the system of men having several wives; wife-beaters; and the education of women.

It is obvious that these beginner cartoonists have a lot to say, and that these grassroots comics give them a voice. By simply photocopying the page that they have made and plastering it on the walls of local shops and other frequently visited buildings, they spread their message and get listened to, maybe for the first time ever.

The examples of comics on these pages are all from India.

▲ A photo from one of the sessions for making grassroots comics by World Comics India. Photo by Sharad Sharma (World Comics India).

दहेज प्रथा

कमलेश सिंह

स्वावलम्बन

◄◄ A story about dowry, where a woman is constantly harassed for not having any. She seeks help from the Commission for Women and the culprit is soon caught and justice is served. Story and art by Kamlesh Singh.

◄ A story of self-reliance among women. These women collect money and use it to start their own fishery. The money they make is then used to build a small library for children in their village. Story and art by Geetanjali Devgum.

◄ ◄ *Card Captor Sakura* by the female collective calling themselves CLAMP from 1996. This is a great example of the genre "magical girl," telling the stories of girls gaining magical powers and using them to fight evil.

◄ A true international comic: *Princess Ai* by American singer Courtney Love, Japanese artists Ai Yazawa and Misaho Kujiradou, and DJ Milky (pseudonym for the American Stu Levy). This shoujo manga is a fantasy story, loosely based on the life of Courtney Love, featuring another outspoken, outgoing, and independent female hero.

◄ ◄ *The Rose of Versailles* by Riyoko Ikeada is one of the earlier and very influential shoujo manga. The story takes place during the French Revolution and the hero Oscar François de Jarjayes is a woman who dresses as a man, thus managing to explore all the thrills of being a man. Translation by Fredrik L. Schodt.

◄ *Princess Knight*, made from 1954 to 1968 by Osamu Tezuka, is seen by many as the starting point for what has become the largest comics culture by and for women: shoujo manga. It tells the story of a young princess who has to pretend she is a boy in order to protect the throne of her kingdom. This storyline has resulted in cross-dressing and transgender themes being popular in shoujo manga.

Girl Power, Manga Style!

I have stated several times in this chapter that the number of female artists working in comics is limited compared to the number of male artists, and that this results in a small proportion of female comics readers. This is true for two out of the three major comics cultures of the world—Europe and America—but not so for the third, Asia. In the dominant Japanese comics culture, a much larger percentage of the artists making comics are female and consequently so are a larger part of the readers.

Comic books have existed in Japan, both for girls and boys, since the early twentieth century, but the Japanese comics business as we now know it didn't really take off until the post-World War II era. The artist Osamu Tezuka revolutionized visual storytelling and created the basis for what is today the largest comics market in the world. In these early years, the stories were geared towards a younger, general—that is to say male—audience. Tezuka was something of a megalomaniac though, and wanted to corner all parts of the market, so he soon started making comics directly for female readers with, for example, *Ribon no Kishi* (*Princess Knight*) from 1954. Soon other artists, almost all male, also got into this market, and a lot of comics for female readers were produced in the following decade.

By 1970, a whole generation of female readers had grown up and started making their own comics, and they quickly outsold their male counterparts. Some of the most talked-about female cartoonists of this period—artist such as Hagio Moto, Yumiko Oshima, and Keiko Takemiya—became known as *hana no nijū yon nen gumi*, or the 24 Year Group, so-named since many were born around the Japanese year Shōwa 24, the twenty-fourth year in the reign of Emperor Shōwa (Hirohito), or 1949. This group and others from this time ushered in a new revolution in the comics market of Japan, taking women's comics to a whole new level,

experimenting with content and form, adding new subgenres, and diversifying comics for female readers almost to the same level as in shonen manga, or comics for boys.

Since the mid-1970s, shoujo manga (comics for young female readers) has been created almost exclusively by women and has evolved into what is perhaps one of the most advanced forms of visual storytelling in the world, using sophisticated layouts and visual symbolism to tell stories in the most efficient and engaging way. The creators of shoujo manga have also branched out, following their readers as they grow up, and there are now subgenres like shonen-ai, yaoi, and josei for older female readers.

All this has led to Japanese comics becoming chock-full of female main characters; characters that are self-reliant, confident, heroic, prone to take action, and all in all a far cry from the Western comics stereotype of women as secondary characters, whose sole purpose is to be a pendant to a male main character. I do not know if this has been a conscious effort of the cartoonists, in order to empower the young readers and make them more self-reliant in the still very conservative Japanese society, but looking at the popularity of these comics and the social changes happening in Japan, it has almost certainly contributed.

The power of these comics also became evident when they were exported to the rest of the world. Suddenly a whole new group of readers of comics emerged: women. Booksellers across the Western part of the world were flabbergasted when female customers were seen queuing to buy comics. And right now a new generation of artists is emerging in many Western countries, and—you guessed it—they are also women, creating manga-inspired comics with strong, outspoken, independent female heroes.

▲ The massive (eight hundred-page) *Office YOU* is one of many Japanese comic books with stories geared towards more mature female readers. This so-called josei manga tends to be more sedate than the more adventurous shoujo, but still contains stories by and for women.

PIRACY IS LIBERATION

BOOK 002: INFOTRIP

MATTIAS ELFTORP

Chapter 7
Political Persuasions

The series *Piracy is Liberation* by the Swedish artist Mattias Elftorp is a political statement disguised as a cyberpunk comic. This is the cover of the second issue out of six published to date. The cover image was produced by the artist Susanne Johansson.

Comics and Politics

Politics is a topic that most will easily associate favorably with comics, rather than some of the earlier themes of this book, such as war, religion, or sex. Still, the persistent misconception of comics being only for children has laid obstacles in the way of cartoonists wanting to include political messages in their comics.

There is a long tradition, running back several centuries, of political cartoons, though. Now these may or may not be deemed "comics," but they at least use a lot of comics' distinguishing features, such as iconic characters, the combination of words and images, and speech balloons. This has spilled over into "regular" comics and may be one reason why politics and this medium seem to go rather well together.

Political cartoons were—and mostly still are—published in daily, weekly, and monthly newspapers and magazines. This is also the medium for one traditional form of comics: the comic strips—which are at least sometimes allowed to be political. Classic examples like *Bloom County*, *Doonesbury*, *Mafalda*, and *Pogo*, and more recently *Boondocks* and *Get Your War On*, demonstrate that you can have an open political agenda and still be a success in this otherwise often rather streamlined part of comics culture.

There is also, of course, the notion that almost everything in life is politics, in some shape or form, the argument being that you cannot create anything—comics included—without sending a political message of some kind. In this chapter, however, the focus will be on more obvious, blatant political propaganda—simply because it's more fun to look at! Finding examples of this is not hard, since politics in many ways is equivalent with persuading people of your agenda, and through the years many have realized the potential of the direct communication that comics provide.

These political comics have been published in different forms in different parts of the world. In the U.S., where the dominant format has been the comic book, there is a long-running history of making special comics books to promote a certain issue, standpoint, or even a specific politician in an election. As the understanding of the medium has changed from being just for kids, politics have also become more and more prevalent in comics in general, as can be seen in how many times Barack Obama has shown up in comics since he started making a name for himself during the presidential campaign.

In the French/Belgian tradition, politics have often been treated using parody within established comics. *The Adventures of Asterix* is a good example of this, where the scriptwriter Goscinny wrote some pretty serious contemporary political satire into what otherwise was a humorous adventure comic set in the distant past. Today, there are specially produced albums, the preferred publishing format in the French/Belgian comics culture, with specific political objectives, like promoting one of the candidates in the latest election for president in France.

In Japan the question of politics in comics is even more complex, not least when looking at the media through translations into Western languages, which is just a small fraction, mostly comprised of commercially oriented comics. There are political comics in Japan, designed specifically for this purpose, but the majority of examples I have found are rather in the context of otherwise fictitious storylines and based on the personal beliefs of the cartoonist working on a particular title. The freedom that the system allows the cartoonists in Japan, including that creators own the comics they work on, allows for a lot of politics seeping through in what would otherwise be deemed as pure entertainment. And then there are the ones that are more obvious, like the recent *Manga Kenkanryu* (*Manga: The Anti-Korean Wave*) by Sharin Yamano, which is a vicious attack on anti-Korean sentiment in Japanese society.

▶ *Historieboken* (*The History Book*) was produced by a group of young Swedish artists who wanted to show the history of Europe and Africa, not as it was usually told in traditional history books, but from a Marxist perspective. The book combines collage techniques, prose texts, and comics, often rather crudely done, but brimming with enthusiasm. All in all, this book, which was done by people who really didn't know how to do a book, sold more than 70,000 copies, and was translated into seven languages.

▶ A political cartoon from 1828 by the Englishman George Cruikshank. Despite the fact that this is almost two hundred years old, the form is just about the same as in political cartoons in the twenty-first century, and the joke could just as easily be used by a cartoonist today.

◀ *Varoomshka* was a comic strip by New Zealander John Kent that ran in UK newspaper *The Guardian* from 1969 to 1979. It has been called the first British political cartoon strip, and it utilized every opportunity to display the heroine's scantily clad body as British political life was satirized.

▼ In two consecutive issues (#39 and 40) from 1944, the magazine *True Comics*—"TRUTH is stranger and a thousand times more thrilling than FICTION!"—showcased the stories of presidential candidates Thomas "Tom" E. Dewey and Franklin D. Roosevelt. These were both propagandistic in the way they presented the candidates, seemingly not favoring either.

▶ Captain America debuted in 1941, and from the start he went for the total patriotic effect, clad all over in the red, white, and blue stars and stripes, and with an "A" on his forehead for those who were still in doubt as to what he symbolized. His sidekick, Bucky, also sported a red and blue costume.

▶▶ In *Fighting American*, published in the 1950s, creators Simon and Kirby made fun of a lot of the clichés they themselves had created in *Captain America* a decade earlier, adding the theme of the Communist scare. Here the heroes battle Poison Ivan and Hotsky Trotsky.

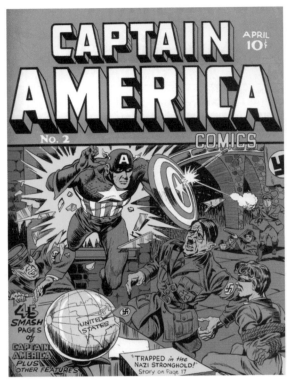

◀ This is one of several propaganda comics published by the American Legion, an influential American organization for wartime veterans. It tells the reader about the history of the American flag, how to display it, and treat it with respect. Created in 1993, it is still for sale through the Legion's website.

▲▶ The Shield is a name that has been used for several characters since the first one was created in 1940. All have worn costumes based on the American flag.

Wearing the Flag

The American flag is one of the most potent symbols on the planet. What it symbolizes depends on the personal beliefs of the viewer, but from the fervent flag-waving of patriotic Americans on the Fourth of July to public flag-burning in countries where hatred of the U.S. is abundant, the power of the symbol remains.

It is inevitable that this symbol would be used in that most American of all genres: superhero comics. Innumerable superheroes have donned garments inspired by Old Glory, ranging from the most well known of them all, Captain America, to the very esoteric and strange. Most of these fictional heroes stem from the same period, the Golden Age of American comics, which is usually said to have occurred around the time of the Second World War. This was a period when patriotic sentiment was not only looked upon favorably, but was almost mandatory within all parts of society, including comics. Thus, a great number of heroes were created who wore red, white, and blue in various combinations.

One of the very first characters to wear these patriotic colors was the Shield, created in 1940 by writer Harry Shorten and artist Irv Novick for the publisher MLJ, which is now known as Archie Comics. The Shield was a man imbued with superpowers after having been exposed to certain chemicals, fighting for the patriotic cause. When this character was overshadowed by Captain America, who in many ways was a duplicate of the original Shield, the comic was canceled.

Captain America is the most famous patriotic superhero. Created in 1941 by Joe Simon and Jack Kirby in a magazine named after the character, he was an instant success, selling one million copies a month, at a time when *Time Magazine* sold 700,000 copies, obviously tapping into the public's desire for a hero to triumph over all evil in the world. When World War II ended, the public's interest in the character waned, and it was not until the 1960s, when Stan Lee resurrected him as a human anachronism, a hero looking for a reason to exist in a more complicated era, that he again became popular. Since then Captain America has never really gone out of fashion; most recently he was used as the main character in very patriotic comics sent to the American troops in Iraq in the twenty-first century.

Simon and Kirby, who left *Captain America* in 1941 due to a disagreement over royalties, created a parody of the character in the 1950s: the Fighting American. His adventures often imitated those of Captain America, but in these post-WWII years, they were imbued with satire and irony. The name of the secret identity of the Fighting American, Johnny Flag, clearly showed the intent of the creators.

Many of the characters created during the Golden Age are resurrected every now and then, making sure that the superhero genre never runs out of characters clad in red, white, and blue. New visually patriotic heroes are also created, even though it can be hard to make them break through and reach a wide audience. One recent example is *Liberty Girl* by Heroic Publishing, which debuted in 2006. Billed as "America's Bronze Goddess of Freedom," this character was even given an origin stating that she was actually from WWII, but has not caught on despite her very revealing dress . . .

EASY NOW, SOLDIER--MOM'S APPLE PIE AND A CUP OF JOE ARE ONLY 50 YARDS NORTH--

Guilty, Guilty, Guilty!

◀◀ The fact that Senator John McCain, since then runner-up in the presidential campaign of 2008, wrote a foreword to a collection of *Doonesbury* was a twist not many had expected, as he had been one of the strip's most ardent critics.

◀ Real-life politicians are often depicted as symbols in *Doonesbury*. The indecisive Bill Clinton, for instance, was made into a waffle after a popular vote by the readers. George Bush, Jr. was initially depicted as invisible, with a cowboy hat, which was later changed into a Roman military helmet. As the war in Iraq got worse, the helmet slowly deteriorated.

When writing about politics and comics, there is no getting around *Doonesbury* by Garry Trudeau. Since its inception, *Doonesbury* has been commenting on politics and blurring the lines between comic strip and political cartoons just like its predecessors *Li'l Abner* and *Pogo*. And it has been very successful at it, angering politicians and even getting a Pulitzer Prize in recognition. The politics in *Doonesbury* are often quoted as being liberal or leftist, depending on who is commenting. This is not strange, considering *Doonesbury* started out as a strip in a university student newspaper in politically volatile 1968. In 1970 it became syndicated, starting with about two dozen newspapers, a figure that has grown to include about 1,400 newspapers all over the world, making it one of the most potent comments on politics in comics ever. Many newspapers have recognized this and have moved the strip to the editorial pages.

Never shying away from a hot topic, *Doonesbury* has continually tested the limits of what can be done in a newspaper strip, angering readers, politicians, and editors. One of the first examples of this was during the Watergate scandal in 1974, when Trudeau had the character Mark, who was a journalist on the campus radio station, do a "Watergate Profile" on John Mitchell (United States Attorney General during the Nixon administration), ending with him exclaiming, "That's guilty! Guilty, guilty, guilty!" This led to a number of newspapers removing this strip and *The Washington Post* running an editorial criticizing it, but it also led to Trudeau receiving the Pulitzer Prize.

Doonesbury has a big cast of recurring characters, something that is quite unusual for a comic strip. On the website, there are twenty-four listed, and since 1984 they've also grown older in real time. This means that today, many of the characters have children attending college, giving Trudeau a whole new chance to poke fun at the American educational system.

▼ A recurring character in Doonesbury is Mr. Butts, used to make fun of the tobacco companies. Here he meets a symbol of pot-smoking, and when they compare the results, Mr. Butts is accredited with 400,000 dead Americans in a year, but Mr. Jay can only say that he caused 735,000 arrests.

► Trudeau made a running gag out of the internet hoax of a study that showed Bush, Jr. had the lowest IQ of all U.S. presidents, having Bush being proud, thinking that it was a high score. In a later strip, the characters asked for forgiveness for this, saying, ". . . we deeply apologize for unsettling anyone who was under the impression that Mr. Bush is, in fact, quite intelligent."

► The (in)famous strip from 1974, where then-United States Attorney General John Mitchell was accused of being "Guilty, guilty, guilty!" This was also the title of the collection, issued later with the strips about the Watergate Scandal.

The strip also features some real-life U.S. politicians, often represented with symbols rather than caricatures. To start with, they would simply appear offstage, but soon Trudeau began using symbols, which has become one of the distinguishing features of *Doonesbury*. George Bush, Sr., for instance, started out as invisible, a comment on his denials of knowledge in the Iran-Contra Scandal. George Bush, Jr. was shown the same way, but with a cowboy hat (because he was a former governor of Texas). Following the controversy over the vote-counting during the presidential election in the year 2000, Bush Jr. was changed into a giant asterisk and the hat was later changed into a Roman military helmet when the Iraq War began.

Trudeau has commented on all the wars that the U.S. has been involved in since the start of the strip, and his liberal ideas have not garnered him many friends in the more conservative parts of the country. Indeed, Senator John McCain denounced Trudeau on the floor of the Senate in 1994, stating, "Suffice it to say that I hold Trudeau in utter contempt," a quote that ended up as the title to the next *Doonesbury* collection. That McCain didn't stop reading Doonesbury is evident, though. In 2005 the foreword to the *Doonesbury* collection *The Long Road Home* was written by McCain, who was impressed with the way Trudeau had treated the subject of seriously injured soldiers, having one of the main characters lose a leg in the Iraq War.

Doonesbury is always on the alert, always commenting on what is going on in the U.S., and Trudeau can always be relied upon never to take himself too seriously. When *Doonesbury* was awarded the Pulitzer Prize in 1975, the Editorial Cartoonists' Society passed a resolution condemning the decision. Trudeau, after checking that the prize could not be revoked, supported the resolution.

Reagan's Raiders!

Ronald Reagan was a politician who stirred everybody's emotions. Whether you were for or against him and his policies, few were left unaffected. Reading the introduction to the very first collection of the long-running political comics magazine *World War 3 Illustrated*, it becomes clear that the magazine was started in 1979 to protest against Reagan. The title was a reference to the looming future that the editors Seth Tobocman and Peter Kuper foresaw when Reagan was running for president, and it is of course not hard to find comics that are directly critical of Reagan in that same magazine. In fact there is even an entire issue (#8) devoted to him, and it's not exactly fan fiction.

A totally different view of Reagan can be found in the outrageous comic book *Reagan's Raiders* from 1986. This was an ongoing title that lasted three issues, written by Monroe Arnold—better known as an actor in various TV series—and drawn by Rich Buckler and Keith Royster. The premise for this comic book was that Reagan, along with members of his cabinet, were secretly transformed into hulking superheroes, clad in suitably tight-fitting spandex in the right trinity of colors and sent on patriotic missions where a square jaw and fists of iron were seemingly the solutions to everything.

The funny thing about this comic book is that it's quite hard to work out whether the creators were trying to make the then-president look silly, or macho. For instance, in the second issue, our heroes take on the entire drug problem in the U.S. by going to South America and attacking a drug lord and his production facilities, fists swinging. Comparing this with the intelligent way Dennis O`Neil and Neal Adams treated the same question in *Green Arrow/Green Lantern* almost two decades earlier, where the creators showed that this is a

much too complicated issue to be rectified by spandex-clad self-proclaimed "heroes," *Reagan's Raiders* is an oversimplified, gung-ho story. Add to this the "War on Drugs" that the Reagan administration waged (and some say lost), and the question of whether scriptwriter Arnold was trying to portray Reagan in a positive or a negative way becomes even trickier to decide.

In issue three, Reagan and his gang set out to complete the ultimate patriotic act of bringing back American POWs from Vietnam. As they rescue their own undercover agents (Rhombo and Schwartzenheimer . . .) and a few American soldiers, and in general manage to issue just about every possible heroic stance, they make utterances like, "I can't wait to meet those cong pigs . . . snout to snout! And hear them squeal!" Considering Reagan's reputation with his political opponents of being almost a fascist, this was probably welcome as a heavy political satire, although at the same time it could also appeal to the followers of Reagan.

So, is it a parody? Certainly! Is it satire? Definitely! But is it propaganda, one way or the other? Well, reading *Reagan's Raiders* now, it is, as mentioned, not clear whether the creators thought this comic book showed the folly of Reagan's macho image, or if they thought that this was going to go down well with the admirers of Reagan. Both interpretations are available on the web. The only thing everyone seems to be in agreement on is that the comics suck!

A more recent treatment of Reagan in comics form is the graphic novel *Ronald Reagan: A Graphic Biography* by Andrew Helfer, Steve Buccellato, and Joe Staton from 2007. The authors have set out to be unbiased and present an objective version of the life of Reagan. I tend to think that they succeeded, but reading reviews from readers with obvious right-wing political leanings, it is clear that the image shown is not to their liking. To them it's left-wing propaganda. As usual, it's all in the eye of the beholder.

Background illustration **Our heroes to the rescue. Seeing not only Ronald Reagan, by then eighty-something, but also Dick Cheney, Caspar Weinberger, and George Bush, Sr., going at it in spandex is enough to turn anyone off the superhero genre.**

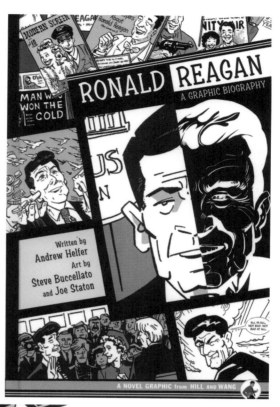

◄◄ *Reagan's Raiders* is one of the weirder comics ever published. This Superman-inspired cover, with the American flag in the background, the eagle on his chest, the bandana with the American colors, and the belt buckle with the insignia "U.S." just about says it all.

◄ The author's attempt in this recent comics biography of Ronald Reagan to show an unbiased view is indicated by the cover, showing Reagan's face split in two parts; one white and smiling, one black and smirking. Whether they succeed is open for debate.

◄◄ In the magazine *World War 3*, the editors and cartoonists Peter Kuper and Seth Tobocman were very clear about their feelings for Ronald Reagan. This example is from 1981 and shows that Reagan was building a great war robot, in the shape of a dinosaur, to battle a similar dinosaur from the enemy—a quite obvious allegory of the Cold War.

◄ Ronald Reagan carrying an American POW away from a Vietnamese prison camp, guns blazing. It doesn't get more patriotic than this.

Anarchy in the UK

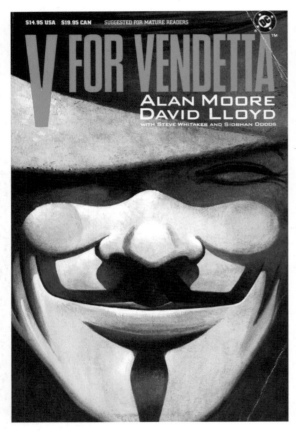

◄◄ The use of the traditional Guy Fawkes mask was the idea of artist David Lloyd, an idea that Moore immediately realized as being a stroke of genius, building a lot of the symbolism of the character V around it.

◄ Here the character V is seen having a discussion with the statue of Justice on top of the central Criminal Court of England, often referred to as the Old Bailey. The symbolism of blowing up the statue of Justice is of course obvious, both to the citizens in the story and for the readers of *V for Vendetta*.

◄ In *V for Vendetta*, Moore has the main character V express classical anarchist ideas to the oppressed British people, ideas mostly resembling those of the anarchist thinker Bakunin.

▲ In Moore and Lloyd's dystopian future of the 1990s, fascist groups take over after an atomic war has destroyed almost everything except Great Britain. They are called Norsefire, recalling both the racial theories of Aryan supremacy and perhaps also the British National Front, an ultra right-wing party with the same initials.

Few comics scriptwriters have had as great an impact as Alan Moore. His comics have been constant bestsellers since the mid-1980s, and through them he has reached millions of readers. Moore has himself admitted that he hopes his works might radically change enough people's ideas on a subject, and one of the most persuasive of all his comics is the anarchistic *V for Vendetta*.

For a reference point for *V for Vendetta*, it would not be unreasonable to pull out the novel *1984*. That was also written by a British author, is set in England, and depicts a dystopian, fascist future— a future that is now in our past. *1984* was written by George Orwell in the post-World War II years as a warning against totalitarianism, a path that Orwell saw just might lie ahead even for his own Great Britain. Moore wrote *V for Vendetta* during the 1980s, seeing the effects of Margaret Thatcher's Conservative rule over Great Britain.

Moore created *V for Vendetta* together with the artist David Lloyd, and it is indeed a bleak future they present in this graphic novel. After a nuclear war, Britain is seemingly one of the few places on Earth still remaining; radioactive fumes cause the national production of food to decrease radically, which leads to civil unrest and eventually to

governmental control by a fascist party. Calling themselves Norsefire, they set up a totalitarian regime, helmed by a leader with complete power. Moore has created a beautiful allegory of the marriage of state and society, with different branches of the Orwellian repressing state named after body parts; the detective branch is called the Nose, the visual surveillance is the Eye, the audio surveillance the Ear, and so on.

Against this effective controlling and subduing organization stands the character V, always clad in a Guy Fawkes mask. His identity is never revealed throughout the story, indicating that he might be the embodiment of anarchy, rather than a specific person. V challenges the fascist rule of Britain and finally brings it to its knees as he kills off leading figures inside the controlling organization, blows up symbolically important buildings, removes the camera surveillance, and gives speeches about anarchy to the scared and subdued people.

Considering that Moore himself has stated that he is an anarchist, it is interesting to look at how closely his ideas are in accordance with those of the character V. *V for Vendetta* was, of course, one of Moore's earliest works, written when he was fairly young, but reading through a recent interview carried out for the book *Authors on Anarchism*, it is clear that, although modified by age and experience, his views are still largely the same. And re-reading *V for Vendetta*, looking for clues, it is evident that although Moore never intended for V to be a classical hero, in depicting the fascist rulers as greedy, perverted, and cold-blooded, he makes sure where the reader's sympathies lie.

That the theme of *V for Vendetta*, which was created as a comment on Thatcherism in England in the 1980s, is still pervasive today, is evident in the way the movie adaption, which was released in 2006, differs from the comic. Actually, when rewriting the story to suit the twenty-first century, so much was changed that in interviews Moore wonders why the director of the movie didn't simply do an original story about the sad state in which George Bush's presidency had left the U.S., instead of hiding behind his comic script.

▶ Perhaps inspired by the use of the mask of Guy Fawkes in *V for Vendetta*, protestors have begun donning replicas of this mask in preparation for demonstrations. In 2008, a group of people demonstrating against Scientology were seen wearing this mask, something that pleased Alan Moore.

Prison Comics

Comics can be used to communicate just about anything, and in many countries comics have been the medium of choice when the aim has been to reach out and touch the hearts and minds of readers. Some comics have been produced by people in jail, such as the comic book *Doing Time* by the Japanese artist Kazuichi Hanawa, showing the mind-numbingly boring existence of Japanese prison life as experienced by the artist after he was arrested for owning a gun (a punishable offense in Japan). Or there are the comics by Mumia Abu Jamal, an American death-row prisoner who was supposedly framed by the police and told his side of the story in the magazine *World War 3 Illustrated*.

The most touching and at the same time most openly propagandistic of all comics about prison life is without a doubt *On afamme bien les rats!* (which translates roughly as *They starve the rats, don't they?*) by the Moroccan artist Abdelaziz Mouride. In the 1960s, Mouride was a founding member of the left-wing movement called March 23 in the politically repressive monarchy of Morocco. This eventually led to him being imprisoned as a political prisoner in 1974. At first he was sent to Derb Moulay Chérif, a famous torture center in Casablanca led by the infamous Kaddour Yousfi. There he was subjected to horrendous torture followed by a mock trial, where he was sentenced to a twenty-two-year-long incarceration. In 1980, he and his fellow inmates began a hunger strike, which led to Mouride acquiring not only a neurological disorder that made it impossible for him to coordinate his movements, but also going blind. For Mouride, who had worked as an illustrator and journalist, this was the ultimate horror.

Eventually Mouride recovered and, wanting to record what was happening, decided to draw autobiographical comics. He drew the pages in prison and had them smuggled out one by one in order to show the world how he and other political prisoners in Morocco were treated. The comics were collected as a graphic novel, which was published in France in 1982 in Arabic and called *Fi 'akhsha'i baladi* (*In the Bowels of My Country*),

with the subtitle *On Political Prison in Morocco*. It was also released in a French version, titled *Dans les entrailles de mon pays*, translated by Mouride's fellow inmate, famous Moroccan poet Abdellatif Laabi. Two years later, in 1984, Mouride was released, twelve years early. This was in all likelihood partly due to his comics, even though they were published using a pseudonym, but also due to the changing times in Morocco.

Mouride himself had no copies of the comics that he made and went on with his life as best he could. The book had a life of its own, though, and was copied and recopied, going around the world. It was read by Jimmy Carter, former U.S. president, and ended up at the United Nations and in practically all major human rights NGOs. Finally, in 1999, Mouride met an American professor from the Massachusetts Institute of Technology (MIT) who was doing research on the writings of political prisoners in Morocco. Mouride told his story to her, regretting that he didn't have a copy left to show, to which she responded that she did! Seeing his comics for the very first time in fifteen years, Mouride was struck by the power of the story and decided to redraw some of it, adding new material and finally having it published in Morocco as *On afamme bien les rats!* in the year 2000.

Reading *On afamme bien les rats!* is a grueling and moving experience. The simple, often rather crude style of Mouride and the personal, diary-like tone of the text adds to the feel of authenticity. Had this graphic novel been done in a slicker, more commercial style, the effect would certainly not have been the same. The strange title is a reference to the hunger strike that Mouride and his fellow inmates undertook. They had gotten accustomed to the presence of rats in the holes in the floor, which were ceremoniously called "toilets," and were saddened when they realized that their strike also deprived the rats of their food.

Mouride is now a leading figure in the burgeoning Moroccan comics scene.

◄◄ The Moroccan edition of Mouride's tragic and touching tale of imprisonment, torture, mock trials, and so on. That it wasn't published in Morocco until the year 2000, eighteen years after publication in France, says a lot about the political climate in Mouride's home land.

◄ The depiction of torture, although not dominant in the book, leaves a lasting impression on the reader.

◄ Other stories from behind bars: *Doing Time* by the Japanese Kazuichi Hanawa, and *"Yard In!"*, a story by Mumia Abu Jamal, an American on death row.

September 11

Nothing has been as momentous in twenty-first-century American history as the attacks of September 11, 2001. As with the assassination of John F. Kennedy, everyone remembers where they were when they heard the news, and this does not only apply to U.S. citizens but to people all over the world. What happened also changed so many things concerning the relationships between the U.S. and the rest of the world that it can be seen as one of the defining moments of this still very young century.

Of course, it also made its mark on comics. Soon after 9/11, comics started to appear that commented on what had occurred. Publishers put together comics anthologies with everything from autobiographical accounts of first-hand experiences of the attack to political statements, from the outright nationalistic/patriotic to the

more critical. Looking at all of these comics from the period after 9/11, they speak of many different interpretations of what happened, and also of the desire to communicate these interpretations.

Many of the earliest comics were patriotic, rallying in defense of the survivors, the police, and firemen of New York City and the U.S. in general. Some of these can be found in the three books *9-11: September 11, 2001 (Artists Respond)*, *9-11: September 11, 2001 (The World's Finest Comic Book Writers & Artists Tell Stories to Remember)*, and *9-11: Emergency Relief*, published by DC Comics, Dark Horse, and Alternative Comics respectively. These are anthologies and the comics are varied, but the general ideas that come across are disbelief, sorrow, anger, and patriotism. Some voices are raised to stave off the retaliations and escalations of violence, domestic and international,

▲ Pretty soon after 9/11, three anthologies were published in support of the emergency services and to come to terms with the agony that had been caused by the attacks. As

can be seen by the covers, these books were mostly supportive of the cause and not very questioning of the politics behind what had happened.

▲ Here Peter Kuper uses a combination of a very graphical representation of his connection with the Twin Towers, and the transformation of a radio broadcast into the famous radio broadcast by George Orwell to achieve a sense of his feelings at this moment in time.

► An example of the comics that Art Spiegelman produced for his project *In the Shadow of No Towers*. As can be seen, this was a highly personal and very political vision of America during and after 9/11.

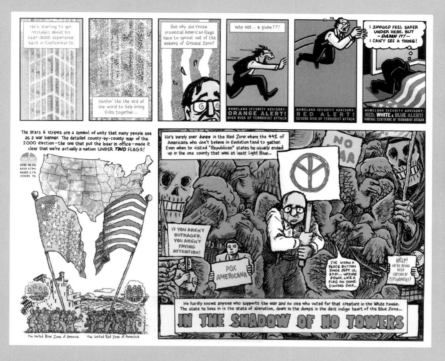

▲ Not surprisingly, *World War 3 Illustrated*, an anthology that in its own words "made it our mission to shine a little reality on the fantasy world of the American kleptocracy," was one of the few early comics publications that contained openly critical comics, discussing the way America had turned after 9/11. Cover by Peter Kuper.

but the general feel is that of support for the system. This was even more obvious in the publications by Marvel Comics: *Heroes*, *The Amazing Spider-Man* #36, and *A Moment of Silence*, all published shortly after the attack.

More openly critical views were presented in the New York City-based anthology *World War 3 Illustrated*, which devoted its thirty-second issue to the attack. Here the editors Peter Kuper and Seth Tobocman, political cartoonist Tom Tomorrow, and several other New York artists gave their view of what happened, or as they themselves expressed it: "We are not trying to prove a point. We are asking questions. Trying to make sense out of the incomprehensible. Looking for our humanity in the rubble." Still, there is a lot of politics in this issue, and it is mostly not in favor of George W. Bush and the way he handled American politics before and after the attack.

Another voice of criticism, calling for a more balanced look at what had happened, was Art

Spiegelman's and his *In the Shadow of No Towers*. This was made in the form of broadsheets inspired by the old full-page comics in American newspapers. All in all there were ten of these, retelling the memory of the day of the attack from Spiegelman's perspective, but also adding the political aspect of the events that occurred after the attack and the hindsight made possible by the fact that the comics were produced between 2002 and 2003. Spiegelman is openly critical of George W. Bush and states that the then-president used 9/11 as an excuse to attack Iraq, among other things. This did not go down well with American newspapers. *In the Shadow of No Towers* was originally published in the German newspaper *Die Zeit*, and then repeatedly reprinted in other major European newspapers. In America, though, only smaller newspapers dared touch it. Considering that Art Spiegelman himself lives in New York and is one of the world's most respected cartoonists, having received the Pulitzer Prize for his work *Maus*, this speaks volumes about the different views on the topic in America and in Europe.

The "Comic" Side
of the European Parliament

Background illustration
**The idea of the EU, a
parliamentary structure
that represents almost
all of the countries in
Europe, is presented
with wordless images
in the very beginning
of the story.**

▲ The book *Troubled
Waters* was designed as
a standard French comic
album, which is a large
hardcover folio format.

▲ The hero of the
comic alternates between
being a bureaucrat and
a private investigator,
à la Sam Spade.

▲ The makers of *Troubled Waters* tried to teach readers about how the EU is run, sneaking bits of facts into the story inconspicuously. Here is a scene that shows how discussions in the Parliament are simultaneously translated to all the languages used by member states.

▲▲ One obvious theme that the authors wanted to get across to the readers was equality of gender, making the MEP a woman and her assistant a man. How common this combination is among the members of the European Parliament is not clear, though.

Most European countries have their own specific comics culture, based on different historical, social, and cultural backgrounds. Even so, one set of comics has been considerably dominant: the French *bande dessinée*, or *BD* for short. Comics from France have been heavily exported to other European countries since the 1930s (especially to Germany) and have also influenced other cartoonists all over Europe. In France, comics were early on regarded as a serious art form and not as something only meant for kids.

Therefore, it wasn't surprising that when the European Union decided to run a campaign to promote awareness of what it does, comics was the chosen medium. Not only that, but they also chose the classical French format for presenting comics: the album, with its large folio format, color pages, and hardcovers.

The European Parliament wanted the comic to be based on an actual case, and one that could at least potentially stir the imagination of the readers. The choice fell upon a resolution from September 2000 concerning water policy, and a request for proposals was sent out, adding an imposing documentation of the resolution at a mere six hundred pages. . .

That the chosen submission came from a communications agency says quite a lot about this process, and sadly it says a lot about the result as well. Granted, it was a heavy undertaking, since the comic book *Troubled Waters* was supposed to inform as well as entertain. The people working on the project—Dominique David, Rudi Miel, and Cristina Cuadra García—are all good at what they do, but the demands of the parliament simply killed the minimal potential this comic had of ever entertaining anyone. The only fun part about it is the main character, Irina Vega, a Member of the European Parliament (MEP) who seems to be a cross between Lara Croft and Nancy Drew—which led some parliament members to point out that they don't actually do much super-sleuthing.

This was a big undertaking from the European Parliament, and the comic has been published in all of the official twenty-two languages of the EU, giving it a total print run of 1,250,000 copies, most of which were given away free. The fact that it is as dull as dishwater tells us it was probably money not well spent.

Civil War and the Patriot Act

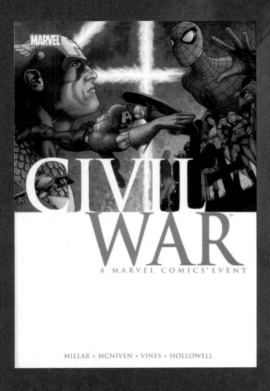

◀◀ The storyline *Civil War* was one of the biggest selling comics of 2006/2007 and with the numerous collections, trade paperbacks, and hardcovers, it reached an even larger number of readers.

◀ *Civil War* is full of allegories. Here Daredevil, who has just been caught, gives Tony Stark, a.k.a. Iron Man, a silver dollar, alluding to the money Judas allegedly received for betraying Jesus.

Superhero comics are not merely the dominant comics genre in the U.S.; they are also a genre that lends itself readily to all kinds of political allegory. Using the sometimes silly concept of having costumed heroes running around saving the world to tell stories about what is actually happening in our real world is not uncommon. In fact, most stories told in the superhero genre resonate with the world in which they were created.

It is therefore not so strange that one of the biggest, most talked about, and well-read storylines so far in the twenty-first century, *Civil War*, can be read as a comment on a lot of things that have been going on in the U.S. the last couple of years.

Civil War was a so-called crossover, which is a storyline that runs through several of the titles of a certain publisher, in this case Marvel Comics.

The main series, simply called *Civil War,* was written by British writer Mark Millar, drawn by Steve McNiven, and published in 2006–2007. The concept this series was built upon was a theme that has been used several times before: that ordinary people living in a universe populated with superhumans might be rather wary of their ability to destroy entire buildings and in general wreak havoc. Millar's new take on this was to introduce the idea of a Superhero Registration Act, a law that says that all superheroes must register, reveal their secret identities, get proper training, and become a kind of governmentally controlled super-police. The story in *Civil War* focuses on the choice this leaves the superheroes and super-villains with, resulting in two opposing teams: one backed by the government and led by Iron Man, and one acting in secrecy and, in a reversal of expectations, led by the ultimate patriotic superhero, Captain America.

◄◄ One of the pivotal moments of *Civil War* is when Peter Parker reveals himself as Spider-Man in order to comply with the new Registration Act ,and lead the way for other heroes to also "do the right thing."

◄ At the end of *Civil War*, Captain America, the leader of the resistance to the Registration Act, surrenders, as he is overpowered not by other superheroes but by ordinary people. A powerful political allegory.

▼ "Whose Side Are You On?" The tagline for the series *Civil War*, invoking a feeling of them and us.

The whole series can of course be seen as a comment on America after 9/11 in general, and more specifically on the USA PATRIOT Act. The Patriot Act, as it is more commonly known, is an American law enforced in 2001, shortly after the attack on the Twin Towers in New York City. It gave American agencies working to prevent terrorism more possibilities when it comes to tapping telephone and email communications, and looking at medical and other documents. It also gives law enforcement authorities greater powers to detain and deport immigrants, among other things.

Many have criticized the Patriot Act, saying that it was rushed through the system using what happened on 9/11 as an excuse. Most problematic for many was that it redefined the term terrorism to also include domestic activities, thus giving the law a much larger area in which it can be enacted. When *Civil War* was written, the Patriot Act was up for reauthorization, meaning it was heavily debated in public forums. It is quite clear that this inspired Millar.

Millar himself stated that the whole story is a political allegory, and even though he tried to give both sides equal billing, it is quite evident where his sympathies—and those of the authors working on the other Marvel titles that were involved—lay. It is possible to read *Civil War* as simply another superhero story, with loads of colorful heroes going for each other's throats, but reading it in the context of the political background at the time gives it a whole other meaning.

▼ During the presidential campaign, IDW published two comics called *Presidential Material*, with flip-covers giving you the biography of both candidates.

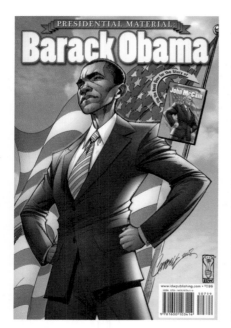

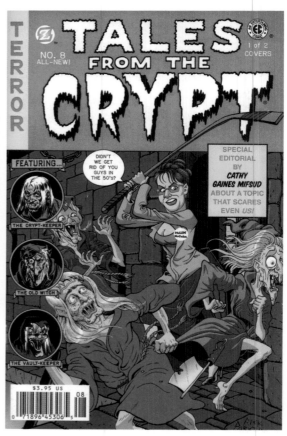

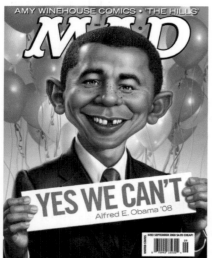

◄◄ The cover of *MAD Magazine* traditionally features caricatures of famous people, real or fictitious, as variations of the magazine's traditional mascot, the hapless, toothless Alfred E. Neuman. Obama was treated to this dubious honor during his presidential campaign.

◄ In the graphic novel *08: A Graphic Diary of the Campaign Trail*, journalist Michael Growley and artist Dan Goldman retold the highlights of the presidential campaign, using photos to speed up the process so that they were able to publish it when the interest was still at a peak.

Yes We Can't!

SHEESH! GUY GETS ELECTED AND SUDDENLY HE'S EVERYWHERE!

◀ **One of the stranger comics to allude to the presidential campaign in 2008 was** *Tales From the Crypt*, **which featured a cover with Sarah Palin bashing the classic characters from the publisher EC. This was an obvious remark on the 1950s, when EC was put out of business by self-appointed moralists (see pages 90–93), and the fact that Palin had been part of banning books when she was governor of Alaska.**

Background illustration **When Marvel Comics decided to play on Barack Obama's rumored collecting of Spider-Man comics, and put him on the cover of an issue of** *Amazing Spider-Man*, **they could not have foreseen that this would become the bestselling single issue, two months in a row.**

In the heat of the U.S. presidential campaign in 2008, everything about Barack Obama seemed newsworthy. Among the revelations published in this media frenzy was the fact that he once had been an avid fan of Spider-Man. Now, large parts of the comics community, as with so many other parts of the cultural scene, were quite possibly already supporters of Obama, but this may have been what tipped the scales. Not in the election, but in the comics.

Obama was featured in a lot of comic books during the presidential campaign. One example was a biography from the publisher IDW, which introduced his and the other candidate, John McCain's histories, backgrounds, and views— *Presidential Material: Barack Obama* (by Jeff Mariotte and Tom Morgan) and *Presidential Material: John McCain* (by Andy Helfer and Stephen Thompson). The creators of these two books tried their best to be impartial, and succeeded pretty well. Both books became bestsellers, but the fourth printing of Obama's version now also includes the President's inaugural speech.

Since it became obvious that there was money to be made in political comics biographies, another publisher has created comic books on women in politics called *Female Force*, with books focusing on Hillary Clinton, Michelle Obama, Condoleezza Rice, Princess Diana, Sarah Palin, and Caroline Kennedy. The design is very similar to IDW's successful covers.

Both presidential candidates were obviously mainstays of political cartoons during the election year, but McCain did not receive the same exposure in comics as Obama. Republican Vice President nominee Sarah Palin did get to be on the cover of *Tales From the Crypt*, but considering the way she was depicted it is debatable whether this was an honor or not.

But when your face adorns the cover of *MAD Magazine*, you know that you are someone to be reckoned with. In the autumn of 2008 Obama was the cover star of *MAD*, and like so many before him, as a version of the magazine's iconic figure Alfred E. Neuman. This was not as far-fetched a combination as might be expected, as the face of the presidential candidate and *MAD*'s dentally challenged figurehead mixed beautifully.

During the campaign, there were also a number of issues of the superhero comic book *Savage Dragon* where the cover image clearly took the side of Obama: "I'm Savage Dragon and I endorse Barack Obama as President of the United States!" This was not the first time creator Erik Larsen had used his comic book to proclaim his political thoughts. During the U.S. elections in 2004, Larsen let his main character run as a candidate, which among other things led to a cover where Savage Dragon beats up George Bush. During the 2008 election, fans asked Larsen if Savage Dragon would be a candidate again, but Larsen simply stated that this was not necessary when there was Obama.

Since the election, there have been even more Obama sightings in comics. Marvel Comics, the owner of Spider-Man, did a short story in *Amazing Spider-Man #583* about how Spider-Man repels a threat to the inauguration ceremony. The sales for this issue reached staggering numbers, and it was the bestselling single comic book in America for two months straight, eventually racking up sales to make it the bestselling single issue so far of the twenty-first century.

Whether any of these comics made a difference during the campaign, or during Obama's time as president is of course hard to say.

Picture Credits

All images are copyright © their respective copyright holders and are shown here for historical and review purposes. Every effort has been made to credit the copyright holders, artists, and/or publishers whose work has been reproduced in these pages. We apologize for any omissions, which will be corrected in future editions, but hereby must disclaim any liability.

108: Treasure Chest of Fun and Facts © The Cathetical Guild Educational Society
110: Francis © Marvel Comic Group and Franciscan Communication Office of New York
Réveille ton coer © Editions des Béatitudes, 1992
111: The Savage Dragon © Erik Larsen, 1996
The New Adventures of Jesus © Frank Stack
Chip Grant © unknown
112: The Most Spectacular Stories Ever Told © DC Comics, 1975
Menneskesønnen © Peter Madsen and Det Danske Bibelselskab, 1995
113: Picture Stories from the Bible © William Gaines Agent, Inc.
The Manga Bible © Siku, 2007
114: Chick Tracts © Jack T. Chick LLC
116-117: The Crusaders © Jack T. Chick LLC
118: The Life of Pope John Paul II © Marvel Comics
119: Battle Pope © Funk-O-Tron, LLC, 2000
The Life of John Paul II in comics © Edizione Piemme S.p.A, 2005
The Life of Pope John Paul II © Marvel Comics
120-121: Hansi: the Girl Who Loved the Swastika © Tyndale House Publishers and Maria Anne Hirschmann, 1976
The Cross and the Switchblade © David Wilkerson and Flemming H Revell Company, 1972
122-123: Archie's One Way © Archie Enterprises, Inc., 1973
124: The Gospel according to Peanuts © Robert L. Short, 1965
The Parables of Peanuts © Robert L. Short, 1968
The Gospel according to Andy Cap © John Knox Press, 1973
The Man from Krypton © John Wesley White, 1978
Good News from Grimy Gulch © Judson Press, 1977
The Gospel According to Superman © John T. Galloway, Jr., 1973
125: Peanuts © Charles M. Schulz
127: Treasure Chest of Fun and Facts © The Cathetical Guild Educational Society
128-129: Amar Chitra Katha © Amar Chitra Katha Pvt Ltd
130: Hairy Polarity © Tim Todd Ministries, 2004
132-133: Bringing up Father © King Features Syndicate, Inc.
134: Bizarre Sex © Kitchen Sink Press, 1977
What a woman may be and yet not have the vote © unknown
Dykes to Watch Out For © Alison Bechdel
135: Prism Comics © Prism Comics, 2003
136-137: Bringing up Father © King Features Syndicate, Inc., 1940
The Smurfs © Peyo and Cartoon Creation
Mickey Mouse © The Walt Disney Company
Blondie © King Features Syndicate, Inc., 1968
Fantastic Four © Marvel Comics, 1961
Background image Donald Duck © The Walt Disney Company
138: Wimmen's Comix © Last Gasp
139: Comic © Trina Robbins
It Ain't Me Babe, interior art © Trina Robbins
It Ain't Me Babe, cover © Last Gasp
Twisted Sisters © Diane Noomin, 1991
140-141: Abortion Eve © Chin Lyvely and Joyce Sutton, 1973
Who Murdered Clarice? © Jack T. Chick LCC
142: Sex Education Funnies © Lora Fountain, 1972
143: Sins of the Flesh © Bobby London, 1972
"Strawberry" Fields and "her old man" © Robert Crumb and Bobby London, 1972

Fat Freddy gets the clap © Gilbert Shelton, 1972
Trots and Bonnie © Shary Flenniken, 1972
144: AARGH! © Mad Love Publishing Ltd., 1988
The Mirror of Love, cover © Alan More and José Villarubia, 2004
The Mirror of Love, interior art © Alan Moore, Steve Bisette and Rick Veitch, 1988
From Homogenous to Honey © Neil Gaiman and Bryan Talbot, 1988
145: Real Dream © Art Spiegelman, 1974
146: FAQs © Sharad Sharma
Comic © Swati Singh
147: Comic, left © Kamlesh Singh
Comic, right © Geetanjali Devgum
Photo © Sharad Sharma
148: Card Captor Sakura © CLAMP, 1998
Princess Ai © Tokyopop Inc. & Kitty Radio, Inc., 2004
The Rose of Versaille © Riyoko Ikeda
Princess Knight © Osamu Tezuka
149: Photo © Fredrik Strömberg, 2009
150-151: Piracy is Liberation © Mattias Elftorp and Susanne Johansson, 2006
153: Historieboken © Elmqvist, Jönsson, Langemar, Rydberg
Varoomshka © Eyre Methuen and John Kent, 1972
Political cartoon © George Cruikshank, 1828
True Comics © True Comics, Inc., 1944
154: Captain America © Marvel Comics
Fighting American © Joe Simon and Jack Kirby, 1989
Our Country's Flag © Custom Comics Service, 1993
The Shield, left © Red Circle Production, Inc., 1983
The Shield, right © Red Circle Production, Inc., 1984
155-156: Doonesbury © Garry Trudeau
159: Reagan's Raiders © Solson Publications, Inc., 1986
Ronald Reagan: A Graphic biography © Andrew J. Helfer, Steve Buccellato and Joe Staton, 2007
160-161: V for Vendetta © DC Comics Inc. 1988, 1989
163: An afamme bien les rats! © Tarik editions, 2005
Doing Time © Kazuichi Hanawa and Ponent Moon, 2000
"Yard in!" © Mumia Aba Jamal and Gregory Benton, 1994
164: 9-11: September 11.2001 (Artists respond) © Dark Horse Comics, Inc. 2002
9-11: September 11.2001 (The World's Finest Comic Book Writers Artists Tell Stories to Remember) © DC Comics, 2002
9-11: Emergency relief © Alternative Comics, 2002
War of the Worlds © Peter Kuper, 2001
165: World War 3 © World War Three Illustrated, 2001
In the Shadow of No Towers © Art Spiegelman, 2004
166-167: Troubled Waters © European Parliament, 2002
168-169: Civil War © Marvel Comics, 2007
170-171: Presidential Material © Idea and Design Works, LLC, 2008
MAD © MAD Magazine, 2008
Tales from the crypt © William M. Gaines Agent, Inc., 2008
08: A Graphic Diary © Michael Crowley and Dan Goldman, 2009
Amazing Spider-Man © Marvel Comics
176: Grenada © A. C. Langdon

Index

Acknowledgments

Writing a book is always a collaborative effort and so was this, even though only one author is named on the cover. I would like to thank all of you who have assisted me on this long and bumpy road, especially my always helpful colleagues on Comics Scholar Group and the Platinum Age Group. Many have given advice this last year or so and helped me find rare items and odd facts, which has enriched the book immeasurably. I would especially like to thank those of you who have loaned me objects to include in the book: Caj Byqvist, Paul Gravett, Christian Kindblad, Nils Kroon, Ola Nilsson, Peter Stanbury, and Germund on Wowern.

I am also deeply indebted to Lotten Peterson, for proofreading, giving me many interesting ideas and for having the inspired idea to go to Cuba just when I was looking for material from that part of the world.

Last, but certainly not least, this book would not have been written if it were not for my beloved Hanna, who valiantly stood by me, corrected my bad spelling day after day and never complained when I sat hours upon hours, neglecting house and family to get this book written.